"I am delighted by the opportunity to learn about Maria Gabriella and her remarkable life, so poignantly documented in her letters and in the notebooks of Mother Pia. Lavich's English translation flows smoothly, and I found myself easily caught up in the gripping events of her life. The book was difficult to put down, as I felt simultaneously dismayed yet joyful, but most of all compelled to continue forward on my own spiritual journey. As a researcher of Italian female saints, this book is a must-read. If you love saints, then you'll love this book."

> — Molly Morrison
> Associate Professor of Italian
> Ohio University

"Add Blessed Maria Gabriella to the list of great monastic letter writers of the twentieth century like Merton and Leclercq. In this volume of her letters she emerges from the cloister with the clarity, sensitivity, and preciousness of St. Thérèse of Lisieux. One need not be a monastic to fall under her spell of love and devotion to both God and the monastic way of life."

> — Deacon Mark Plaiss
> Author of *No End to the Search: Experiencing Monastic Life*

MONASTIC WISDOM SERIES: NUMBER FIFTY-SEVEN

The Letters of Blessed Maria Gabriella with the Notebooks of Mother Pia Gullini

Translated by
David Lavich, OCSO

Bl. Gabriella Sagheddu

Introduction by
Mariella Carpinello

α

Cistercian Publications
www.cistercianpublications.org

LITURGICAL PRESS
Collegeville, Minnesota
www.litpress.org

A Cistercian Publications title published by Liturgical Press

Cistercian Publications
Editorial Offices
161 Grosvenor Street
Athens, Ohio 45701
www.cistercianpublications.org

Interior photos are from the archives of the Trappistine Monastery of Vitorchiano, Vitorchiano (Viterbo), Italy. Used with permission.

© 2019 by Order of Saint Benedict, Collegeville, Minnesota. All rights reserved. No part of this book may be used or reproduced in any manner whatsoever, except brief quotations in reviews, without written permission of Liturgical Press, Saint John's Abbey, PO Box 7500, Collegeville, MN 56321-7500. Printed in the United States of America.

Library of Congress Cataloging-in-Publication Data

Names: Gabriella Sagheddu, 1914–1939, author. | Lavich, David, translator.
Title: The letters of Blessed Maria Gabriella with the notebooks of Mother Pia Gullini / translated by David Lavich, OCSO.
Description: Collegeville : Cistercian Publications, 2019. | Series: Monastic wisdom series ; NUMBER 57 | Includes bibliographical references.
Identifiers: LCCN 2018046333 | ISBN 9780879075576 (pbk.)
Subjects: LCSH: Maria Gabriella, 1914–1939,—Correspondence. | Gullini, Maria Pia, 1892–1959.
Classification: LCC BX4705.M3866 A4 2019 | DDC 271/.97 [B] —dc23
LC record available at https://lccn.loc.gov/2018046333

Table of Contents

Preface   vii
   by David P. Lavich, OCSO

Photographs   xiii

Introduction   1
   by Mariella Carpinello

The Letters of Blessed Gabriella   47

Autograph Notebooks of Mother Pia Gullini   143

Mother M. Pia Gullini and Sister Maria Gabriella   167
   by Maria Paola Santachiara, OCSO

Doing Nothing, Achieving All:
Blessed Maria Gabriella of Unity   193
   by Mark Scott, OCSO

Bibliography   209

Contributors   215

Preface

Even a cursory survey of monastic literature will soon reveal that most of it is an exposition of the wisdom teaching or spiritual theology of abbots and abbesses. Consider the Desert Fathers and Mothers or the great abbots and abbesses of the twelfth- and thirteenth-century monastic world. What they said or wrote, although intended primarily for the members of their community, eventually attracted the attention of many outside the cloister, including academic theologians and even popes. Their theology, which was never seen as a separation from their lived spiritual experience, influenced the shape and flavor of their times, especially the medieval church. Indeed, this literature continues to inspire and engage a diverse spectrum of people today.

This being said, it is obvious that most of the ordinary monks and nuns remained in the shadows, convinced of the apostolic fruitfulness of their hidden monastic life. This conviction of course corresponds to Saint Benedict's Rule for Monasteries: "If in fact speaking and teaching are the master's task, the disciple is to be silent and listen" (RB 6.6). In the Cistercian tradition and especially within the Trappist context, this silence that fosters prayer and interior recollection was observed continually, and consequently little is known of the lives or personalities of the individual monks or nuns except what may have been noted about them and kept in the archives of their monasteries.

Sometimes, however, a light shines out from the shadows of the cloister and catches the attention of people far beyond the monastery. Such is the case of Blessed Maria Gabriella Sagheddu, who died in 1939 at the Italian Trappist monastery of Grottaferrata (which was transferred to Vitorchiano in 1957) at the age of twenty-five years, after having offered her life for the cause of Christian unity. Pope Saint John Paul II referred to her as "Gabriella of Unity" and proposed her as an example of spiritual ecumenism, referring to her in paragraph 27 of his encyclical *Ut Unum Sint* of 1995:

> Praying for unity is not a matter reserved only to those who actually experience the lack of unity among Christians. In the deep personal dialogue which each of us must carry on with the Lord in prayer, concern for unity cannot be absent. Only in this way, in fact, will that concern fully become part of the reality of our life and of the commitments we have taken on in the Church. It was in order to reaffirm this duty that I set before the faithful of the Catholic Church a model which I consider exemplary, the model of a Trappistine Sister, *Blessed Maria Gabriella of Unity*, whom I beatified on 25 January 1983. Sister Maria Gabriella, called by her vocation to be apart from the world, devoted her life to meditation and prayer centered on chapter seventeen of Saint John's Gospel, and offered her life for Christian unity. This is truly the cornerstone of all prayer: the total and unconditional offering of one's life to the Father, through the Son, in the Holy Spirit. The example of Sister Maria Gabriella is instructive; it helps us to understand that there are no special times, situations or places of prayer for unity. Christ's prayer to the Father is offered as a model for everyone, always and everywhere.[1]

In light of the fact that the monastery of Grottaferrata was poor economically and somewhat lacking in cultural resources, something emerged that is both refreshing and unexpected.

---

[1] Pope John Paul II, *Ut Unum Sint*: On Commitment to Ecumenism, http://w2.vatican.va/content/john-paul-ii/en/encyclicals/documents/hf_jp-ii_enc_25051995_ut-unum-sint.html.

At a time in Italy and beyond when the word *ecumenism* was hardly known, this monastery became a pioneer center of prayer for unity as well as an established partner in contacts with non-Roman Catholic Christians, mostly because of the wise and forward-thinking abbess, Mother Pia Gullini. Furthermore, unknowingly, Sr. Gabriella's self-offering of love for the church became a focal point of interest and enthusiasm for the cause of unity.

Christians devoted to ecumenism will naturally be interested in the letters of this simple nun, whose name will always be linked with the cause of ecumenism. Others will intuit from these letters to her family and abbess that here is something honest, true, heroic, very human, and very spiritual. Perhaps that is because an authentic pure love stronger than death always astonishes us. Another point of interest might concern Sr. Gabriella's relationship with her abbess. Little has been written about such relationships in the context of an enclosed monastic community of women. Here the reader can discover the strength and delicacy of two very different women determined with all their might to go together straight to the goal.

Other than an interest in the personality of a saint, what can these simple letters of Gabriella transmit to us? If this is monastic literature, what can it teach the reader? Perhaps we can take a clue from the first sentence of the first letter of Gabriella to her mother that appears in this volume. Here we read of her arrival at the Trappist monastery at Grottaferrata: "With great pleasure I write to you to let you know that I arrived at my destination." It would later be revealed how truly she did arrive at her destination, which was to live in the heart of the church that will, in God's time, be united. Running with all her strength and love, she reached her goal with the unfailing help of her mentor, Mother Pia. And she can teach others how to do the same. Her message is that the way to self-fulfillment is self-donation; only a love stronger than death will satisfy.

In his apostolic exhortation on the call to holiness, *Gaudete et exsultate* (#5) of March 19, 2018, Pope Francis cites Blessed

Maria Gabriella as an example of holiness through the gift of her life for the cause of unity: "The processes of beatification and canonization recognize the signs of heroic virtue, the sacrifice of one's life in martyrdom, and certain cases where a life is constantly offered for others, even until death. This shows an exemplary imitation of Christ, one worthy of the admiration of the faithful. We can think, for example, of Blessed Maria Gabriella Sagheddu, who offered her life for the unity of Christians."[2]

The monastery of Vitorchiano testifies to an increased interest in Blessed Gabriella in the English-speaking world, building a relationship with some Benedictine Anglican monasteries in England, particularly Mirfield, and correspondence with people in the USA, Australia, and the Philippines. This English edition of the *Letters* follows on the French and Spanish editions. The French edition, published by Abbaye Val Notre-Dame Editions, appeared in 2010: *Lettres de la Trappe—Gabriella de l'Unité*. The Spanish edition, *Cartas desde la Trapa—Beata Ma Gabriella Sagheddu*, appeared in 2015 from Editorial Monte Carmelo.

Professor Mariella Carpinello, who is the editor of the Italian edition and author of the Introduction to this volume, is a proficient writer on women's monastic history and spirituality. She has the advantage of being close to the subject both culturally and through familiarity with the monastic community of Vitorchiano. Professor Carpinello's research into the archives of Vitorchiano offers to the reader the fruit of her professional work. It is doubtful that the *Letters* as presented in this volume could be understood without all her helpful background references and information in the introduction. The remarks jotted down by Gabriella's abbess in her *Notebooks* in response

---

[2] Pope Francis, *Gaudete et exsultate*: Apostolic Exhortation on the Call to Holiness in Today's World, http://w2.vatican.va/content/francesco/en/apost_exhortations/documents/papa-francesco_esortazione-ap_20180319_gaudete-et-exsultate.html.

to inquiries about Gabriella prove a valuable insight into her personal character and virtue as witnessed by the person who was spiritually the closest to her.

Similarly, Sr. Maria Paola's article quotes extensively from both the *Letters* and from Mother Pia Gullini's *Notebooks* as well as from other archival materials. Her own experience as seen and lived from inside Bl. Gabriella's present-day community of Vitorchiano brings an added enrichment to this volume. Undoubtedly her acquaintance with some surviving nuns who knew both Mother Pia and Bl. Gabriella is invaluable. Finally, the article by Dom Mark Scott, abbot of New Melleray Abbey in Iowa (United States), brings to this volume an insight into the relevance of the subject viewed at a distance from its European context.

The reader of this volume will quickly discover that this is not just a story of a young woman who died at an early age of tuberculosis in a Trappist monastery. No disease and no one took her life from her. She gave her life, and she didn't bargain to take it back. Gabriella understood her self-offering as made to God and accepted by him for the sake of the unity of his church—the whole church, the whole body of Christ. In a time of increasing national, political, and faith-related divisions, she remains as a silent prophet of unity and peace. This is not an invitation to others to make an offering of one's life in the same way that she felt called to do; that would be foolish. Nevertheless, it is an invitation to join her on the road that leads from division and brokenness to unity. As a monastic teacher Gabriella demonstrates that faith, hope, and love are more powerful than clever arguments or unyielding positions, and it is a love stronger than death that wins out in the end.

Acknowledgments

I am indebted to Dr. Mariella Carpinello, editor of the Italian edition of the *Lettere dalla Trappa* and author of the Introduction of this volume, and to Sr. Maria Paola Santachiara, OCSO, for their agreement to this English translation of their work. Thanks also to Dom Mark Scott, abbot of New Melleray Abbey, Iowa, USA, for his willingness to have his article appear in this volume.

I am also grateful for the assistance given to me by Professor Roberto Taglienti, instructor of the Italian language in Rome, for helping me decipher some challenging Italian expressions, and to Sr. Kathleen Riley, OCSO, of the Abbey of Vitorchiano, for assistance in proper English usages.

Special recognition must be given to Sr. Gabriella Masturzo, OCSO, nun of Vitorchiano and Postulatrix for the causes of the saints of the Order of Cistercians of the Strict Observance, for her unfailing and prompt assistance in confirming or seeking further information pertinent to the subject.

Finally, I can only acknowledge with praise and admiration the tireless work of Dr. Marsha Dutton, Executive Editor, Cistercian Publications, for her patience and attention to professional standards as well as the long hours spent in making this volume possible.

David P. Lavich, OCSO

Blessed Gabriella Sagheddu (1914–1939) as she appeared when she arrived at the Italian Trappist monastery of Grottaferrata in 1935. (Photo taken to make her identity card needed to leave Dorgali and travel to the monastery of Grottaferrata.)

Mother Maria Pia Gullini, abbess of Grottaferrata from 1931 to 1940 and from 1946 to 1951.

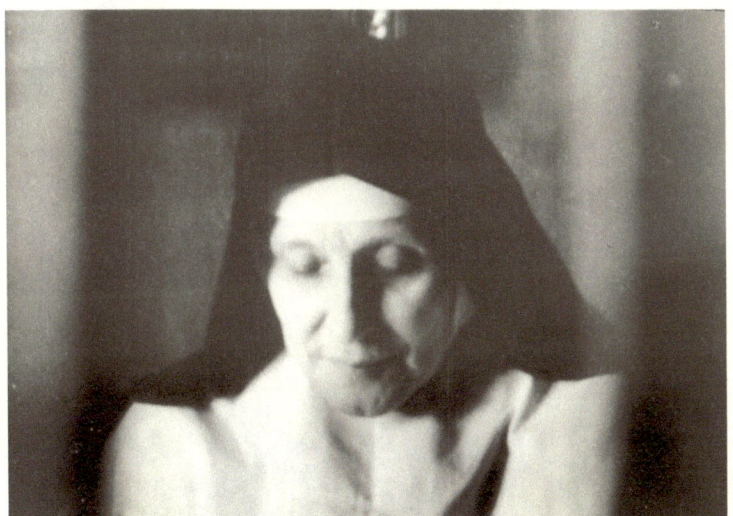

Unity Chapel at the Trappist monastery of Vitorchiano with the urn that contains the body of Blessed Gabriella. (The remains were transferred from Grottaferrata in 1975 and buried in the Unity Chapel after the beatification on January 25, 1983.)

Aerial view of the monastery of Vitorchiano (Viterbo), Italy.

Introduction[1]

Mariella Carpinello

According to Saint John the Evangelist, a few hours before Jesus' arrest, thinking of the disciples and the Christians of future times, Jesus addressed the following words to the Father:

> I do not ask for these only, but also for those who will believe in me through their word, that they may all be one, just as you, Father, are in me, and I in you, that they also may be in us, so that the world may believe that you have sent me. The glory that you have given me I have given to them, that they may be one even as we are one, I in them and you in me, that they may become perfectly one, so that the world may know that you sent me and loved them even as you loved me. (John 17:20–23)

In the small volume of Gabriella Sagheddu's gospel book the page that corresponds to this text is worn from frequent re-readings. Her name is now linked to the same text in the basic acts of the Church dedicated to ecumenical questions. *Gabriella of Unity*: this is the name used by John Paul II when referring to her in paragraph 27 of his encyclical *Ut Unum Sint* of 1995:

---

[1] Translated by David Lavich, OCSO, from the Italian as printed in Gabriella dell'Unita (Bl. Maria Gabriella Sagheddu), *Lettere dalla Trappa*, ed. Mariella Carpinello (Milan: Edizioni San Paolo, 2006). Some section headers in this translation are not found in the original text. Words in brackets are provided by the translator.

> Sister Maria Gabriella, called by her vocation to be apart from the world, devoted her life to meditation and prayer centered on chapter seventeen of Saint John's Gospel, and offered her life for Christian unity.[2]

Sr. Gabriella's story as a nun took place within the secret of a Trappist monastery in the Lazio countryside more than half a century before that encyclical was written.

Her Life

Maria Sagheddu, who took the name of Maria Gabriella in religion, was born on March 17, 1914, in the village of Dorgali, in Sardinia. Imagine the sheer beauty of Sardinia in the early years of the twentieth century, still steeped in its ancient pastoral civilization, celebrated by travelers across the Alps for its archaic features and the harsh yet hospitable temper of its people. Little Maria resembled the natural and human landscape of her homeland: stubborn, impetuous, rebellious, and strong-willed. After her death, when the first scholars came to visit Dorgali in order to construct her biography, her mother, siblings, friends, and teachers all described a girl who was indomitable and had little inclination for religious practices. She herself, after becoming a nun, confessed that in her early years she had been impatient, intolerant, and opposed to anything contrary to the affirmation of her own will. But, in view of her future, we can imagine that this little girl, kicking and agitated, already carried inside her something restless and something incompatible with commonly accepted views, something that placed her in constant collision with her surroundings.

When she was only a few years old, an epidemic of the Spanish flu deprived her of her father, grandmother, and a brother. Certainly those sudden deaths hurt her deeply, as is

---

[2] Pope John Paul II, *Ut Unum Sint*: On Commitment to Ecumenism.

pointed out in the biographies that trace the reasons for her religious sensibility.³ Moreover, early deaths were frequent in those years in the villages of Sardinia, among people still struggling to survive. Every family had its share.

Intelligent and lively, Maria benefited from elementary school until the sixth grade but was then forced by poverty to leave school, to pursue housework and help the family in the countryside. Although encouraged by her mother, she was bored by going to church. Nevertheless she distinguished herself by her generosity in lavishing herself on those in need, even on one occasion for the sake of a woman of ill fame. She was also devoid of malice and allowed herself to be teased without taking offense, having fun laughing at herself. At seventeen years of age, she lagged behind her peers in preparing for Confirmation, but, being older, she prepared with greater mindfulness, and she discovered horizons of interiority previously ignored.

Modesty was so much a part of Maria's nature that the men of the country, congregating at night in the square to watch the girls come up from the river with their washed clothes, complained that they never got to see her eyes. At eighteen she was a naive beauty, silhouetted in the brown colors of the women of this land. In her picture taken for her identity card—which has now become well known throughout the world—we

---

[3] Cf. Celestino Testore, *Suor Maria Gabriella trappista* (Vitorchiano: Monastero di N.S. di S. Giuseppe, 1958); Monica Della Volpe, *La strada della gratitudine: Suor Maria Gabriella* (Milan: Jaca Books, 1983); Paolino Beltrame Quattrocchi, *La Beata Maria Gabriella dell'Unità* (Vitorchiano: Monastero di N.S. di S. Giuseppe, 1983).

English biographies include the translation of the last of these: Paolino Beltrame Quattrocchi, *A Life for Unity, Sr. Maria Gabriella*, trans. Sr. Maria Jeremiah (New York: New City Press, 1990). Further citations of Quattrocchi, however, refer to the Italian original. See also Martha Driscoll, *A Silent Herald of Unity: The Life of Maria Gabriella Sagheddu*, Cistercian Studies Series 199 (Kalamazoo, MI: Cistercian Publications, 1990); and Pearse Cusak, *Blessed Gabriella of Unity: A Patron for the Ecumenical Movement* (Ros Cré, Ireland: Cistercian Press, 1995).

meet her affectionate eyes, which remain rather private; we see the sketches of a smile that does not diminish the seriousness of her expression, at the same time sad and happy. Several opposites make up her face, childish yet aware.

In the same year[4] Maria's seventeen-year-old sister Giovanna Antonia died. Suddenly the turmoil of Maria's character subsided, and Maria began to spend a lot of time in church. She also participated in Catholic Action, which until then she had declined to attend, and which joined together the great ideals launched by Armida Barell: ministry, heroism, and the Eucharist. Above all, her character became gentler. During this period she received some marriage proposals, one of which she kept in reserve for some time before answering, but she finally refused it. Only the pastor of Dorgali, Father Basilio Meloni, knew why. Maria had received her call.

It should be noted that the first step towards the religious life of Maria Sagheddu was well supported by this zealous and well-educated priest, who helped her to resolve the first unknowns. Maria trusted him unconditionally, while he knew how to listen with full respect, recognizing a genuine contemplative vocation, perhaps the vocation most difficult to accept for a mother and family considering the prospect of a drastic and final separation. The first decision to make was where to go to pursue her vocation, but Maria didn't know. She had never been out of her own region. The call that she had received summoned her irresistibly, but the how and where remained unknown. Don Meloni had contacts with the Trappist monastery of Grottaferrata, a hill town of Castelli Romani, and he had already sent a friend of Maria's, Maddalena Fancello, there. So to the question "Do you want to go to Grottaferrata?" she replied, "Send me where you will," and the priest concluded, "You will surely go to Grottaferrata."[5] With those few

---

[4] Actually apparently the next year, when Gabriella was eighteen (ed.).

[5] Concerning the relationship between Gabriella and Father Meloni, see Dionigi Spanu, "La Beata M. Gabriella Sagheddu (1914–1939) nella testimonianza del suo padre spirituale Don Basilio Meloni (1900–1967)," *La palestra del clero*, I, nos. 1–2 (2001): 79–100, here 84.

words, which were sufficient given the trust between them, everything was resolved. A few years later, when the trial of Maria had been completed, Father Meloni claimed to have "that supernatural affection for her that a shepherd of souls has for his spiritual daughters."[6]

It is worth pausing for a moment on this *supernatural affection* intrinsic to the gospels—think of the tears of Mary Magdalene at the empty tomb on Easter morning, as the voice of the Risen One calls to her. We can think of the *apophthegmata* of the Desert Fathers, especially the story of the young John of Lyco, who was ordered by a senior monk to water a stick planted in the sand every day. Without asking the motive for this foolish command, John ran every day for some kilometers in the hot sun to get water and irrigate the dry branch, which after three years bloomed prodigiously. Blind obedience, full of spiritual content, which brought humanity to the era before the rebellion of Adam, would also bear fruit in the case of Maria. Thus Father Meloni, when testifying for her beatification, could write, "I feel reverence for her," explaining implicitly that the submission of this girl did not mean the passivity of the inexperienced before those who know, but faith.

Moreover, the reciprocal roles of these two persons, although functioning in a hierarchy, did not relegate the inferior person to a minor position; rather, it won veneration on the part of the superior. Now this relationship between Maria and Don Basilio Meloni was all the more precious considering that they were living in the mid-1930s, when the Second World War was about to break out, and that during the postwar reconstruction the sense of the value and beauty of such a relationship would be lost even in the spheres of consecrated life. Later generations were to suffer for a long time, consciously or not, from the absence of fathers. For her part, Maria knew that to respond to God, more than making choices and observations, meant entrusting herself to him, and because of this docility,

[6] Spanu, "La Beata," 83.

her entry into religion was easy. Her mother recounts the same thing when saying their final *goodbyes*:

> I remember the day she left; I was crying as I said *goodbye*. Maria asked me the reason for my tears and said, "Why are you crying; aren't you even worthy of having a daughter who is a nun?" And then I said, "Go with God and he will help you." I resigned myself and said, "Rather than return home, God will take you to Heaven." She was walked to the bus only by a cousin who carried her suitcase because Don Meloni would not have been happy if a lot of people had gone there to bid her farewell.[7]

She and her mother were never to see each other again.

Even during the journey Maria felt escorted by her father confessor, who had discerned this [vocation] for her. We find peace in the letter where she describes to her mother the majesty of the Roman churches, which must have looked amazing for a country girl but which nevertheless did not distract her from the confident desire she had to arrive early at her destination.

Finally Maria reached the Trappist monastery of Grottaferrata. It was September 30, 1935. She was twenty years old, shining with strength and health, her long black hair gathered in thick braids that surrounded her head like a crown. She wore the traditional costume of Dorgali—a long skirt, jacket, and fringed shawl—in the colors of her country, recalling the sea, the fires of the shepherds, sheep's wool, cork forests, and pastures. The abbess, Mother Pia Gullini, who in her youth had been a fine painter, describes her appearance thus:

---

[7] *Positio super virtutibus, Beatificationis et Canonizationis Mariae Gabriellae Sagheddu, moniale professae O.C.S.O.*, p. 32. This is the document or collection of documents used in the process by which a person is declared Venerable, the second of the four steps on the path to Roman Catholic sainthood.

She was beautiful, but her modesty hid her like a veil. . . .
Her stature was slightly above average. . . . Broad forehead and beautiful, bright large eyes with a deep expression and so transparent that when she came to see me, I had the impression of seeing her soul. . . .
Her mouth was rather large, but her smile had a sweetness, a stunning beauty that revealed her teeth, white and straight, which manifested youth and health. The chin was broad and very strong-willed. Hers was a classic profile.[8]

Maria's first letters home told of her attentive interest when going out to meet situations that she didn't yet understand but that she already loved. Leaving Dorgali without knowing precisely what a Trappistine monastery was, she would soon become a Trappistine because of her careful attention, and, indeed, she would somehow become the very prototype of a Trappistine nun in the eyes of the world.

The Trappist monastery of Grottaferrata, or Grotta, as its name was simplified by these religious—evoking the cave of Bethlehem and the many caves of Western Christianity where monastic life was nestled through the centuries—was one of the most active centers of asceticism on the Italian peninsula. There the Rule of Saint Benedict was observed following the customs and practices of the Cistercian spirituality of Bernard of Clairvaux and the reform of Armand de Rancé, the abbot of legendary rigor who lived at the end of the seventeenth century in the French abbey of La Grande Trappe and was devoted to the primitive austerity of Benedictine monasticism.[9] The regimen of fasting, working in poverty, and spiritual diligence that was maintained at Grotta could not be tolerated by everyone who aspired to it: some postulants were

---

[8] From Mother M. Pia Gullini's "Notebooks" for Gaston Zananiri, biographer of Gabriella, now in the Vitorchiano Archives; see pages 143–66 below.

[9] Anna Maria Caneva, *Il riformatore della Trappa: Vita di Armand Jean De Rancé* (Rome: Città Nuova, 1996).

sent back home, and others chose by themselves to abandon the field.

The history of the Italian Trappistines, which began in the late nineteenth century, unfolds in its entirety from a vocation to this very austerity. Indeed, from difficult beginnings, the lack of resources, and extreme poverty, a community gathered together by the persistence of the French Teresa Astoin on the hill of Saint Vito near Turin was opposed by the bishop, misunderstood by the brothers, and finally transferred to Grottaferrata to be subject to the direction of the neighboring monks of Frattocchie. When Maria Sagheddu entered, the community included some of the old protagonists of that early adventure, which the monastic authorities had declared to be doomed to failure, but from which would come—as had been expected by the courageous founders—an abundant and expansive progeny.[10]

Mother Pia

The abbess of Grotta, as we have seen, was Mother Pia Gullini. Her teaching is inextricably grafted into the story of Gabriella Sagheddu, so that today it is impossible to consider one without the other, although their personalities were poles apart. In temperament, Mother Pia resembles the major figures of Christian history: the heroines of the Old Testament, the founders and the mystics of every season. Like other women who populated the history of Western monasticism, she was also a personification of the Rule, which she embodied without fail; she was a unique personality from whom arose the practice of a vigorous asceticism that did not extinguish the qualities unique to her nature; if anything, they were strengthened. Her biographical itinerary took place under the sign of a fearless acceptance of God's will.

---

[10] For the history of the Italian Trappistines see Monica Della Volpe, *La Strada,* and Mariella Carpinello, *Il monachesimo femminile* (Milan: Mondadori, 2002).

Mother Pia, in the world Maria Elena Gullini, was born in 1892 in Bologna into a family of the upper middle class and received the refined education of the daughters of her class. She lived in Rome for twenty years, cultivating the study of languages, painting, and music, and frequented high society, receptions, court dances, sports clubs, and charities. She often traveled abroad with her father, an industrial manager who held a high position in the Ministry of Communications, in order to open new sections of the railway. Photos of her early youth portray her cutting tricolor ribbons and receiving flowers. A friend, remembering when they first met, wrote that she was "a beauty, of extraordinary elegance, with dress and hat which at that time were called *da carrozza* ('lady in a carriage')." She added: "She was very refined, cultured, and intelligent, with a golden voice, a smile, and a charm which she has always preserved."[11]

In 1916, having refused numerous requests for marriage, Maria Elena decided to enter religion, defining her intention in one sentence: "My way is love." Such a phrase could not be taken for granted in the early twentieth century, when the choice for the cloister still corresponded more to the idea of the deprivation of a penitent rather than to the choice for full happiness. She would discover later that her project was the same as that of Thérèse of the Child Jesus: "As soon as I had in my hands the first publication of the *Story of a Soul*, my joy was at its height. The road on which I had been walking was sure: a 'little sister' had gone ahead, and therefore I would not go wrong."[12]

At twenty-five, Maria Elena joined the renowned Trappist Abbey of Laval, in Normandy. In this French community the young Italian novice with such an exuberant temperament appeared too "eccentric," so many years later some sisters still

---

[11] From a private testimony of a companion of her youth, Archives of Vitorchiano.
[12] Quoted in a manuscript of M. Pia to Sr. Fara Crapanzano, Archives of Vitorchiano.

remembered her unconventional mannerisms with amazement. On the other hand, Maria Elena, who in religion was called Maria Pia, adapted quickly to the needs of Trappist life, which was a good match for her determination. This response could easily be seen in her work on the farm, in doing lowly and sometimes repulsive tasks, and in a series of struggles quite foreign to her life as an elegant young woman who had grown up in comfort, with intense intellectual interests and admired for her charm. But having arrived at her goal of consecration in a luxurious sleeping car, she was then placed overnight in the strict confines of every renunciation.

In any case Maria Elena's adaptation was immediate. Dazzled by love for the God-man, she claimed that the beginnings [of her vocation] included understanding that "to love is to obey" and learning to embrace "the Constitutions and Usages as one embraces Love."[13] Later she noted in her *vademecum*, her handbook, "I did not come to the Trappists because I was attracted by the spirit of penance or the work; no! I came in order to love the Lord better."[14]

Maria Pia's conception of monastic life was very high, even heroic, and she had the gift of transmitting her fervor. Becoming mistress of the lay sisters of Laval, most of whom were peasants from Normandy, she brought them to an ascetic standard they were unable to maintain after she was gone. Vital and indefatigable, her character was reminiscent of the early Cistercians, the founders of Molesme, Cîteaux, and Clairvaux, monks of severe asceticism, serious study, and hard manual work, with an inclination toward mystical joy: able men ready for everything.

In 1926 the major superiors asked the young professed nun to return to Italy, assigning her to the Trappist monastery of Grottaferrata, in the expectation that soon she would become

---

[13] M. Pia Gullini, *Lettere e scritti di Madre Pia*, ed. Ennio Francia (Rome: Messa degli artisti, 1971), 5.

[14] Gullini, *Lettere e scritti*, 149.

the leader. She described her return as a "sacrifice." To leave France, which had always been the great home of Western monasticism, the land of Cluny, Cîteaux, the Grande Chartreuse, the Grande Trappe, and the liturgical revival of Dom Guéranger[15] in the post-revolutionary and post-Napoleonic era, involved a sort of demotion. The differences between Laval and Grotta were considerable, as was women's monasticism generally between the French and the Italians. The French nuns were cultured and lived their charism while taking into consideration their social and secular cultural context, whereas in Italy, women's monasticism was intellectually poor and influenced by a clerical mentality that obscured part of their specific spiritual merit.

Grotta, however, though poor materially and intellectually, was a truly fervent community and was soon ready to rise up in a new direction. When Gabriella entered in 1935, Mother Pia had been abbess for four years and had already imprinted her untiring influence on the community. She had at her side as mistress of novices Mother Tecla Fontana, another extraordinary monastic figure, who came to the contemplative life after spending twenty-five years as a Franciscan missionary in Egypt, teaching Italian in an institute in Cairo. Both Mother Pia and Mother Tecla had returned to Italy after having adopted another country, and so they possessed an understanding of diversity in peoples and mentalities. For both of them, consecration had meant opening themselves to differences. In the internal relationships among sisters, the community, which numbered fifty-four nuns, must have reflected this different, wider appreciation, opposed to exclusive particularisms. For when Gabriella entered she felt well liked not only by the mothers who were the leaders in this hierarchy but also by the sisters (See Letters 1 and 3).

---

[15] See Gregorio Penco, *Il monachesimo frà spiritualità e cultura* (Milan: Mondadori, 2000).

Gabriella's Early Experience at Grottaferrata

At that time monastic communities were still divided between choir nuns and lay sisters, the former dedicated in a special way to the celebration of the liturgy and chanting the Divine Office, while the others were more engaged in ordinary tasks.[16] Mother Pia assigned Gabriella to the choir sisters, though Gabriella would have preferred otherwise. But she assimilated the discipline quickly. Without saying so and perhaps not even thinking about it, she adhered to the customs and usages as one clings to love. The Trappist monastery was her nest, the source from which she was being nurtured, growing up, and waiting to take off, a paradise, the garden of complete fulfillment. Her satisfaction was evident, especially in the letter in which she described to her mother the particulars of her day with the serenity of one who had conformed spontaneously. Thus, at the end of the day that had begun well before dawn, spent between prayer and study, work and meditation, when night fell she seemed to be able to start again afresh (see Letter 8).

Those were the times when Trappists lived in an almost absolute silence, and, when necessary, they communicated with signs. At night they lay down on straw mattresses in the dormitory, where the tiny cells were separated from each other by partitions that did not reach the ceiling. Re-reading the Rule of Saint Benedict, we find the passage describing the monks as night watchmen who anticipate the dawn, an impressive picture unchanged from the Italy of the sixth century, the time of the Gothic invasions, and proposed again at Grotta in the nineteenth century, the time between the two great wars. At the entrance was written a phrase that today might seem out of date: *Asceterio cistercense*, "the Cistercian arena," or place of

---

[16] The division of the community into two classes is foreign to the Rule of Saint Benedict. Adopted in the monasteries of the West in the Middle Ages, especially by the Cistercians, this division was abolished at the time of Vatican II. The Decree of Unification for the Trappists came in 1965.

spiritual combat. After recent decades in which the world had changed so much, it is not surprising that the young heard the contemplative call specifically to monasteries of greater discipline, such as Grotta at that time, when monastic life was understood and carried out in a radical way. Thus the first few letters of Gabriella describe the trepidation of a soul called to complete self-dedication; she found the place to live this out and did not cease to be grateful.

Conscious of human inadequacy, we can only try to imagine her innocent aspirations when she met the monastic tradition: through lessons and liturgy, she personally encountered Bernard of Clairvaux, the great commentator on the Song of Songs and the cantor of divine love. She encountered the feminine holiness that he inspired, which had become a flood of vitality that from the thirteenth century onward invaded the West, with a constellation of monasteries denser than had ever been seen before, or than would be seen later. Moreover, this flood ran through the capacious riverbed of Cistercian mysticism with literary works that, like rivers of karst, nourished Western religious history. Gabriella's encounter with tradition continued with Lutgard of Aywières, who was favored with many insights into creation and the afterlife, renouncing everything to have the Heart of Christ,[17] and with Gertrude the Great, who in over more than a thousand pages recounts her conversations with the Lord and the infinite forms of his generosity.

In addition, among the readings assigned to beginners at Grottaferrata for their formative content and example were books by authors who were not Cistercian or Benedictine, such

---

[17] The author of her first biography was the Dominican Thomas Cantimpré, *Vita Lutgardis*, in *Thomas of Cantimpré: The Collected Saints' Lives: Abbot John of Cantimpré, Christina the Astonishing, Margaret of Ypres, and Lutgard of Aywières*, ed. Barbara Newman, trans. Margot H. King and Barbara Newman, Medieval Women, vol. 19 (Turnhout, Belgium: Brepols, 2008); see also Thomas Merton, *What Are These Wounds? The Life of a Cistercian Mystic, St. Lutgarde of Aywières* (Milwaukee: Bruce Publishing Company, 1950).

as *La vera sposa di Gesù Cristo* by Alfonso de' Liguori and *The Life* of Maria Maddalena de' Pazzi.

What is clear from the letters that Gabriella sent to her loved ones is her pure joy in belonging to that world of holiness and to God. Mother Pia writes of her in this way: "She hardly said anything, but her total gift, her docility, absolute and deliberate, her calm personal equilibrium, humble gratitude, and affection, pure and filial: all this you could read in her eyes."[18]

Gabriella possessed a quality necessary for those who begin the monastic path: the consciousness of the myopia of her personal positions. She had a distrust of herself, so when one of her superiors ordered something, she could no longer think otherwise of the matter. Without looking for questions and explanations, and without resistance, she found her way to simple abandonment. Hers was the acquiescence of a true monk, for whose conquest the Rule envisions an intensive program of spiritual ascesis in the continual exercise of humility, obedience, and silence. And Gabriella's not being able to think otherwise from her superiors[19] was all the more remarkable considering how much attention Saint Benedict devotes to obedience, an obedience that is not only respectful but is also accepted inwardly until it becomes connatural. If we recall the rebellious nature of the girl Maria Sagheddu with her family in Dorgali before the divine call pacified her, this obedience is all the more unexpected.

Because of this new readiness to obey, Mother Pia did not need to worry about Maria, because during the months of the novitiate she never committed real transgressions, only a few minor errors. Of course, for today's prevailing culture, which values individual independence, this twenty-year-old, who was willing to surrender herself, would be suspected of passive fragility and assessed by psychological criteria, whereas, to the contrary, ancient monks would have esteemed her as a

---

[18] Gullini, "Notebooks," p. 146 below.
[19] Gullini, "Notebooks," p. 151 below.

strong woman with the soul of a fighter. Mother Cristiana Piccardo writes thus:

> Even today, confronted with the mystery of a vocation, attention is given to that critical mentality, analytical, often materialistic and calculating, which evaluates, compares, and checks before accepting. However, at the time of Gabriella one dove wholeheartedly into what one found, into the sea of the holy will of God, with no return. And who knows, maybe one touched more quickly the bottom of a genuine abandonment and leapt rapidly beyond the legacy of a thousand anxieties and fears of psychological analysis.[20]

The one shadow hanging over Gabriella in her first year at the Trappist monastery was the fear of not being judged suitable for monastic life, the fear that she might not enter definitively into the place that was for her the house of Christ and her own home. Many consecrated persons have experienced this fear. Even the Benedictine Jean Leclercq, who with his books and lectures reached myriads of readers and lay audiences around the world, and who was certainly one of the twentieth century's more extrovert explorers, also claimed to have suffered in his youth the same fear as Gabriella: the fear of not being accepted in that place confined within itself but full of all possibilities, the cloister. Today nuns and monks of many monasteries tell us the same thing, if we are lucky enough to be able to exchange a few words with them at the boundary of the enclosure: "We well know that fear."

So nothing would have been more unbearable for Gabriella than to return to the world after having witnessed that *beyond* to which she was called, the place into which she wanted to lose herself before even fully knowing it. Then finally the necessary time passed: she completed the novitiate, and the

---

[20] Cristiana Piccardo, "Ritrovare una sorella," in *Alla scuola della libertà: Riflessioni sulla vita monastica* (Milan: Ancora, 1992), 97–133.

rite of profession was set for October 31, 1935. Her personal prayer on that day included, among other things, a sentence announcing and, so to speak, already containing her immediate future: "O Jesus, I offer myself to you in union with your sacrifice." The offering that would follow, that of her life, was to be the consequence of this one; in a way, it was really to be the same offering.[21]

The letter she wrote to her mother for the occasion is among the most significant of her correspondence. It says, among other things:

> The joy that I felt and still feel is indescribable. The world cannot give these joys and therefore cannot understand them either. Only Jesus can make souls experience these intimate joys that make them forget the sorrows of this exile on earth, and that light up more and more in the soul the desire for Paradise. These joys cannot be explained in words; only those who experience them know what they are. Before, I was always afraid that I would be sent away and that my desire to be all for Jesus would come to nothing, but now I am sure that I will always remain in the house of the Lord, and so my joy is immense. (Letter 24)

Since by that time she no longer had to worry about being rejected, full of gratitude she asked Christ to send her any trial, even sickness and death. Even tuberculosis: "Now I am professed: so, Lord, do anything you want now; if you want me to die, or become sick, or even if I become consumptive—although in my family there is no such person—I am ready. Lord I want to be a victim, but you see to it, because you know that I don't know how to suffer."[22] But at the time, nothing

---

[21] Maristella Bartoli, "La beata M. Gabriella Sagheddu," unpublished conferences 2003–2004, Scuola Cultura Monastica del monastero S. Benedetto delle benedettine dell'Adorazione Perpetua, Milan.

[22] Gonario Cabiddu, *Lettere di una figlia scappata di casa* (Sassari: Stamperia artistica, 1982), 134.

could make one think of illness in this young nun; everything lay ahead of her at the golden moment of her consecration.

The Ecumenical Ideal

In the monastery of Grotta, especially in the years when Gabriella entered, something was in motion and being cultivated that was still very alien to Italian consecrated life and to Roman Catholic society in general, namely, the ecumenical ideal. Already there existed a worldwide movement of persons who worked for the union between the Christian denominations and the establishment of a new dialogue with the Jews. One of the first initiatives dates back to 1838, when a group of Anglicans founded The Association of Universal Prayer for the Conversion of England, which soon spread to England, Belgium, Germany, and northern Italy; a few years later it was transformed into the Association for the Promotion of the Unity of Christendom, finding sympathies among the Roman Catholic laity and clergy. It was in this context that the idea of inviting Christians for a week of prayer for unity was born. However, the program contained uncertainty because it implicitly recognized the catholicity of three confessions, the Anglican, the Roman Catholic, and the Greek Orthodox. In 1864 in a letter to the bishops of England, the Holy Office declared that they considered the prayer for unity to be praiseworthy, but they could not support an association that put the three confessions on the same level of doctrine.[23]

With the fundamental question remaining open, namely, whether this unity should happen with the return of all Christians under the authority of Rome, groups began to form that tended to assimilate the cultic practices of the Roman Church; thus Anglo-Catholicism was born, with the consequent proliferation of various new associations. Pope Leo XIII, in apostolic letters issued between 1895 and 1897, encouraged the

---

[23] *Acta Sanctae Sedis* 27 (1894–1895): 65.

work of these groups, and also promoted a geographical bridge between Italy and England by promoting The Association of Our Lady of Mercy in the church of Saint-Sulpice in Paris, destined to spread the ideals of union. In the same period on the other side of the ocean, new experiences arose, such as that of the Episcopal priest Paul Wattson, who founded first a third order of Franciscan men, the Franciscan Friars of the Atonement, and then, together with the Anglican Benedictine Frances Lurana, a women's community in a small convent in Garrison-on-the-Hudson, in upstate New York.[24] At the dawn of the new century, Paul Wattson addressed an invitation to the members of his society to work for the incorporation of Anglicans into the Holy See. In 1907 he launched the initiative of an Octave of Prayer, starting on January 18, the feast of the Chair of Saint Peter in Rome, until January 25, the feast of the Conversion of Saint Paul. The next year he wrote the following in the monthly magazine *The Lamp*, which was founded to disseminate the ideals of union:

> This Octave, for prayer and joint efforts to promote true catholic unity, is particularly fitting because it combines the names of the two great apostles who together founded the Holy Roman Church, which is by divine disposition the center around which all must come together and whose authority everyone must recognize, before the body of the faithful may become one flock under one shepherd.[25]

In 1909 Wattson's communities were received into the Roman Catholic Church. A few years later, in 1916, Pope Benedict XV extended the Octave of Prayer for the whole world. Despite the success of the initiative, many Christians from non-Roman Catholic churches were still reluctant to adopt it because, as it

---

[24] David Gannon, *Father Paul of Graymoor* (New York: The Macmillan Company, 1951), 35.
[25] Charles Boyer, "L'idea di P. Paul Wattson," *Unitas* (1956): 161–65; and *Unità cristiana e movimento ecumenico* (Rome: Universale Studium, 1955), 92–119.

was laid out by Wattson, it contained the explicit recognition of the primacy of the Roman pope.

Another similar core group was formed in the Low Countries under the aegis of Pope Pius XI when in 1925 at Amay-sur-Moise a monk of Mont-César near Louvain, Lambert Beauduin, founded the Priory of the Union for rapprochement with the Eastern Churches. When presenting the work of the monks of Amay, Beauduin wrote, among other things, in the magazine *Irénikon*: "The first objective: to accustom the Christians of the West to unite their prayers to that of Jesus on the evening of the Last Supper, so as to share in this supreme intention that absorbed all of the concerns of the Master at the time of his departure from us, that they might be one, that they might be consumed in unity."[26] It is interesting to note that the then apostolic nuncio in Paris, Cardinal Roncalli, the future Pope John XXIII, knew Beauduin and appreciated his methodology, valuing it as the only viable option. These convictions would be reflected years later in the declarations of Vatican II in the field of ecumenism.

Meanwhile, a close collaborator of Beauduin, the abbé Paul Couturier, a priest in Lyon, in 1937 introduced a significant programmatic turn, proposing a new formula for the Octave, whose prayers would implore the unity of the Church "as God wills it and by the means he wills." He argued that the ways in which such unity would be fulfilled should refer only to God, not to systems developed by human beings.[27] Father Couturier was one of the main representatives of the so-called spiritual ecumenism, which, without ignoring the causes of the divisions, aimed to renew in the hearts of believers the pain of the separation and to inaugurate a new era of reconciliation, harkening back to the gospels. He conceived the movement

---

[26] Reported by Monique Simon, *La vie monastique, lieu oecuménique: Au coeur de l'église-communion* (Paris: Les Éditions du Cerf, 1997), 63–64.

[27] Maurice Villain, *L'abbé Couturier: Apôtre de l'Unité chrétienne* (Paris: Casterman, 1957), 74.

as a single invisible monastery that extended to those involved in ecumenism the world over, all of whom together constituted the first actual Christianity.

Conceived on these principles in January of the same year, the invitation to participate in the Octave of Prayer, still in its unpublished formulation, also reached the Trappist monastery in Grottaferrata.

Mother Pia Gullini came to know the ecumenical ideals during her years in Laval, and she was enthusiastic about them. Reading what the word *love* meant for her—"to fight against character defects, the self, egoism, arguing and insisting on one's own opinion, judging, resisting, and self-assurance"[28]— we can understand why the encounter with Christians of different confessions might have been inwardly easy for her. If, as she claimed, in her youth her way was love, and love means knowing how if necessary to integrate one's personal position with that of others, then her embrace of the separated brethren had already happened before she decided what words should accompany it.

It is no surprise that this nun who had come from Laval to Grotta with sentiments of unity, and who had maintained written correspondence with the exponents of this movement, whose developments in France were very fast, was encouraged not to delay. Therefore, in 1937, when she received from Paul Couturier an appeal that would address a wide audience of believers, she read it to the nuns in their chapter meeting. In the same notice there was also a reference to voluntary offerings made under the safeguard of humility and duly authorized: that is, the personal offering of the individual for this common goal.

After the meeting, a nun of seventy years, Mother Immacolata,[29] met with Mother Pia and requested permission to offer herself for the few days that still remained for her to live. This

---

[28] Gullini, *Lettere e scritti*, 146.

[29] Mario Maccalli, *Madre dell'Immacolata* (Crema, Italy: Artigrafiche Leva, 1984).

nun belonged to the first vanguard of Italian Trappistines, who had established themselves amidst many difficulties on the hill of San Vito near Turin and whose monastery was later transferred by the monastic authorities to Grottaferrata. Originally from a poor peasant family, capable of devotions and renunciations impossible for others, she had spent almost her entire life in the Trappist monastery. The request that she was making now to offer herself was only for permission to make sacrifices in continuity with those she had made in the past. Besides, in her request there was nothing strange, since other people of different nationalities and Christian denominations had already offered their lives for the same cause. Hence she received permission. Years later, to a scholar who inquired about the delicate and difficult issue of self-offering, Mother Pia replied,

> You ask me if the holocaust of one's very life is a Cistercian tradition. I believe it is a need for every generous soul, especially those in the cloister. We have nothing else but ourselves; we have given everything. By our vows we gave ourselves in the normal way; now we would like to place a greater emphasis on the offering, adding to it a meaning of suffering, consummation, and the renunciation of life, with the acceptance of a premature death.[30]

The death of Mother Immacolata, which took place the following month, is pointed out as one of the first events that occurred in Italy in the area of the so-called spiritual ecumenism. Furthermore, not only religious society, but even the consecrated life was still very far from accepting these practices. During those years in the 1930s the relations between Catholics and Protestants were aflame with polemics, so much so that the two parties came to appeal to secular powers for regulating mutual disputes. In the climate of closed minds, Grotta began to radiate toward the Roman world a new sensitivity toward

---

[30] Gullini, "Notebooks," p. 151 below.

the possibility of an exchange between denominations, albeit still in an imprecise manner.

In the year following the death of Mother Immacolata, in January of 1938, a new request for the Octave came to Mother Pia from Father Couturier, entitled "The Universal Prayer of Christians for Christian Unity." It ends, "Without willingly closing our eyes to the differences, attempting to resolve them in a syncretism that destroys true faith, we will try first of all to emphasize what brings us closer. In this way some of the prospects of convergence will come to light, in which will appear the need to deny all that is negative and reevaluate our respective dogmatic approaches."[31] The Octave was celebrated as in the previous year, each day being devoted to those of a determined persuasion: the Eastern Orthodox Christians, the Protestants of Europe, those of America, nonpracticing Catholics, Jews, and pagans around the world.

We do not know just how Gabriella expressed her offering because, although it was customary to leave a written document in such cases, she did not do so. Given that the Trappist life took place in silent reserve, even this decision of hers matured in secret and remains there sealed. If something may have been written during those days in private notebooks before she died, she took the precaution of destroying them, erasing any trace of it. Even afterwards the issue of her Trappist consecration is entrusted to silence.

However much one might intimately wish for it, the gift of self, and any other offering, is not simply a personal choice; the Rule states that no extraordinary individual initiative should take place without the superior's being aware of it. This is not only out of respect for obedience, but because it preserves the sense of human limitations in penances that are not customary, such as was already taught by those champions of mortification, the Desert Fathers. Before offering herself, Gabriella had to ask permission. She spoke first to Mother

---

[31] Quattrocchi, *La Beata Maria*, 128.

Tecla, who, remembering those occasions after many years, wrote:

> In those days Sister Gabriella confided in me about what the Lord was asking: she also wanted to offer her life for the unity of the Church. It was a subject that could not leave me indifferent. After twenty-five years on the missions, I had and I still have among the dissenters [non-Catholics] many souls dear to me, and I could not wish for better than to see them enter the fold of the one good shepherd. But experience had taught me that the great means to achieve this was through prayer and sacrifice. Leaving prayer to me, Sister Gabriella wanted to take on the sacrifice. Could I tell her no? I immediately had the impression that her sacrifice would be accepted and that I had lost a daughter of so many and such beautiful hopes.[32]

Next, Gabriella turned to the abbess. Her attitude was that of a person convinced that she was "doing nothing" and that she had "never done anything," which consequently allowed her to offer herself as a paschal lamb. Considering Gabriella's age, and the fact that this idea might perhaps be the result of youthful recklessness, Mother Pia responded with deliberate indifference, minimizing the situation. When, after a few days, Gabriella insisted a second time, stating that it seemed to be the will of God that attracted her to sacrifice, the abbess referred the solution to the Father Confessor. Then she forgot about it, perhaps considering the fulfillment unlikely.

The Offering

"Since the day I offered myself I haven't felt very well."[33] With these words Gabriella recounted the immediate result of her offering. At first the malaise did not seem worrisome. According to the monastery doctor it was a simple cold;

---

[32] Memoirs of Mother Tecla Fontana, Archives of Vitorchiano.
[33] Notes of Mother Pia, Archives of Vitorchiano.

nevertheless he decided on an X-ray, which would require a momentary exit from the enclosure. Mother Tecla could still recall this—it was in April 1938—when Gabriella prepared to leave her "nest" to go to the hospital of San Giovanni in Rome and submit to examinations, sure to return in the evening:

> Remember, how could I forget? It was in the morning that Sister Gabriella had to go to the hospital for X-rays. Neither she nor we could imagine that they would have kept her in the hospital. That unexpected trip was for Gabriella and for me a painful surprise. The decision was made in just a matter of a few minutes. Reverend Mother sent the dear sister to me for a change of shoes. She didn't know exactly what they wanted to do; she had to go out, but she thought that she would return before evening.
>
> Then she came to me; going out of the monastery was very unpleasant for her, but she did not say a word. She obeyed at any cost. When I asked her to take off her slippers, she looked at me without saying a word and obeyed. Like an echo I sensed the agony of that heart. . . . We looked again without saying a word; then we embraced quietly and she left.[34]

Gabriella did not return that day. The radiological examination found "a condensation of all the upper lobes on the right lung showing a very white central area surrounded by smaller ones . . . an abnormal reinforcement at the base of the lung."[35] The diagnosis was tuberculosis. This discovery was completely unexpected, both because there were no precedents in the Sagheddu family and because it was impossible that Gabriella could have been infected within the walls of the monastery. However, the doctors said they felt optimistic and assured her of a rapid healing with the treatment of pneumothorax because of the small area of the disease as well as the robust constitution of the patient.

---

[34] Fontana, "Memoirs."
[35] See Letter 27, p. 93 below.

For her part Gabriella must have sensed now that things would turn out differently. She had surrendered everything she had, youth, health, and life. No one could know better than she whether her gift had been accepted, regardless of any medical opinion. The disappointment of not being able to return immediately to the monastery was heartbreaking, as she wrote to Mother Pia: "I have cried so much that I cannot cry any more." Even in the following weeks it was not the prospect of the disease running its course that was able to distress her, but being forced to be away from Grotta. The unexpected hospital stay was a return backwards, a collapse into the agitations of the world after having been happily snatched away from it.

We can imagine, though at a distance, her repugnance when we read the chronicle of an observant visitor to Grotta: the surrounding rural landscape, the bareness of the premises, the impression that one had discovered an essential place where every thought contained ultimate meaning. Gabriella had by then taken root in that place and could only feel brutally affected by words—too many, trivial, banal, and incessant—from the other patients. The silence of the monastery: anyone who has listened to it for even a short time as a visitor in the guest house knows how unpleasant it is to become re-accustomed to the noise of the world. Yet for a nun, silence is not desirable merely because of the absence of sound. Among other things, it is the customary language for intimate conversation with God. No other form of religious life, to my knowledge, loves and cultivates this silence as the Trappists do with their austere requirements. The Trappistine Gabriella must have suffered the shattering of silence as if she were undergoing physical violence.

There is a passage in the Rule that summarizes the entire spiritual atmosphere, the passage where Benedict urges the monk "to make oneself a stranger to the ways of the world."[36] Making oneself a stranger to the world is given support in the

---

[36] RB 4:20; *Saint Benedict's Rule for Monasteries*, trans. Leonard Doyle (Collegeville, MN: Liturgical Press, 1948), 15.

monastery—especially when monastic life is as demanding as at Grotta—where all time flows in the direction of the eternal, where consequently the offering of one's life corresponds to that lifestyle, where the ordered rhythm of the day supports a love as all consuming as the love of Christ, and where that love that calls someone to something beyond human strength finds stable ground for support.

In a Trappist monastery, although there are few words, the resources of the spirit are freer, and it becomes possible, perhaps easier, to indulge in the joy that the world cannot give or even understand. For the Trappistine Gabriella, the real problem was not her death looming over her, but the noise in the hospital ward. In a state of unrest, she abandoned herself completely to God, who made her feel as if she were hovering over an abyss. The inability to be recollected, to be nourished by the Word of the Lord at certain fixed hours in the liturgy, the absence from people who could direct her interior life: none of these things made her waver in her purpose, which, as she herself said, she did not regret and had not ever regretted. But it threw onto her shoulders the entire weight of the inestimable act of offering: "My heart is torn, and without special help from heaven, my cross has become so heavy that I can no longer hold up" (Letter 29).

And again: "Sometimes I wonder if the Lord has not abandoned me; other times I think he tries those whom he loves, and yet at other times it seems impossible that God can be glorified by this sort of life, but I always end up abandoning myself to the divine will" (Letter 29).

She began to think that her superiors were heartless because they wanted to cure her at all costs, and she says that she considered herself "a pygmy in the way of the spirit . . . carried about with every wind that blows" (Letter 33). Yet it is precisely that dark night known not only to contemplatives but also to those dedicated to missionary works and believers who seek God in the world, in which the storm ultimately strengthens the spirit now deprived of all human comforts. At a certain point, the young patient reached the goal of that part of her spiritual journey: "now I truly understand that the glory of God and being a victim does not mean to do great things; rather it consists in the total sacrifice of oneself" (Letter 31). This conviction has been expressed for thousands of years by those who live the mystical life.

The Consummation

The pneumothorax treatment was of no benefit to her; in fact it destroyed the last resistance to the disease. Gabriella had left the monastery still rather strong, but when she returned forty days later she was much worse. As she entered the monastery infirmary, which she would never leave, she announced to the Sister Infirmarian that this disease was her treasure, and she would not share it with anyone.

The following year, the last of her life, was spent in physical pain and exhaustion, but she was not discouraged. Perhaps it was especially during these months that Gabriella read and reread chapter 17 of the gospel of Saint John (without being able to imagine that on the day of her beatification a great pope would speak of this), as she tenderly lingered on particularly personal verses, the pages now worn by her fingers. Far from thinking about the developments that were destined to lead to her posthumous fame, she only wanted to be with God, as mystics always long to do. This was also the intention of the young Saint Benedict in his flight from the world, retreating, unbeknown to all, into the hermitage of Subiaco.

It is not only within the cloister to which she belonged that the events concerning Gabriella have been pondered until the present day. During the weeks when she was rapidly deteriorating, a new dialogical bond was formed between Mother Pia and the Anglican Abbey of Nashdom, established in 1926 in the English county of Buckinghamshire, with the express purpose of working for union with the Roman Catholic Church. Although Nashdom belonged to the Church of England, the monks there were in every respect Benedictines, both in the celebration of the liturgy in Latin, according to the Roman rite, and in the general observance of the Rule. The novice master of the abbey, Benedict Ley, had learned from Father Paul Couturier that at the Trappist monastery of Grottaferrata an elderly nun, Mother Immacolata, had died for the cause of unity. After writing in July 1938 to the abbess to express his sympathy, he received from Mother Pia a reply informing him of the offering of a young nun who had fallen ill with tuberculosis and was now dying. Dom Benedict addressed the sick nun directly, communicating his affection and gratitude, hoping, he later remarked, to receive some autographed message from her. But Gabriella did not even consider the idea of responding; she only asked Mother Pia to please say *thank you* in her stead.

Gabriella died on April 23, 1939, at the hour of Vespers. The gospel passage of that day expresses the purpose of her end:

> I am the good shepherd . . . and I lay down my life for the sheep. And I have other sheep that are not of this fold. I must bring them also, and they will listen to my voice. So there will be one flock, one shepherd. (John 10:14-17)[37]

A few days before, Gabriella had become twenty-five years old. Her journey was short, and it finished in full fruition. Recently professed, she never became lukewarm in fervor, nor did she lose her passion. She invested the enthusiasm of her beginnings in embodying the perfection of an ideal, and she put that into practice.

In the golden age of women's spirituality, the twelfth century, Hildegard of Bingen described this moment in life in words that extend to all times: "O virginity, you are in the royal nuptial bed. O, how sweetly ardent in the embrace of the King;

---

[37] On the death of Gabriella, following that of Mother Immacolata, see M. Augusta Tescari, "Radunare tutti i cristiani nell'unico Regno di Cristo," *L'Osservatore Romano*, 14 January 2000.

even when the sun illumines you, your radiant flower never wilts. O noble virgin, never shall the night come unexpected and wither your flower."[38]

The Story of a Biography

On June 30 of the same year, 1939, a Sardinian writer, Maria Giovanna Dore, entered Grottaferrata as a postulant.[39] Mother Pia entrusted to her the project of writing a biography of Gabriella. Such a project is a respected custom whereby the masters and disciples of a holy monk are expected to hand down his memory after death. In this way some of the most fascinating books of monastic literature have been born. One may recall the life of Radegunde, written by Venantius Fortunatus, the poet whom she converted. Dore's book was ready within a year; a well-known Catholic journalist, Igino Giordani, wrote the foreword.

As part of this editorial initiative it is interesting to note Giordani's attention in his introduction to the best aspects of Gabriella and her community. An anti-Fascist from the very beginning, for many years he headed the press office of the People's Party and published books on the principal religious themes dealing with the problem of how to live the Gospel in a society crisscrossed by warring ambitions. He was highly thought of in Vatican circles, and as an expert communicator he was at the forefront of current affairs and social proposals.[40]

---

[38] Ildegarda di Bingen, *Ordo virtutum. Il cammino di Anima verso la salvezza*, ed. Maria Tabaglio (San Pietro in Cariano: Il Segno di Gabrielli, 1999).

[39] Dore left Grottaferrata and became a Benedictine nun and foundress in Sardinia; her first biography of Gabriella is Maria Giovanna Dore, *Dalla Trappa per l'Unità della Chiesa: Suor Maria Gabriella (1914–1939)*, foreword by Igino Giordani (Brescia: Morcelliana, 1940). This was followed by Maria Giovanna Dore, *Suor Maria Gabriella della Trappa di Grottaferrata: Amore e sacrificio per l'unità cristiana* (Rome: Edizioni Paoline, 1940).

[40] Giordani was a journalist and politician, born in 1894. In the first postwar period he headed the press office of the Anti-Fascist People's Party and had connections with the opponents of the regime and with Piero Gobetti.

Trappist monasticism meanwhile remained deliberately in the shadows. The fact that this informed Catholic intellectual did not know about the Trappists suggests that most Catholic intellectuals of his time in general knew little about them. As he himself confessed, he had never seen a Trappist. For most people the very term *Trappist* evoked Tibet and the Far East, as if the West lacked its own inexhaustible treasury of ascetic culture. Writing on Gabriella therefore allowed Giordani to come closer to a reality that, although corresponding to a deep vein of ecclesiastical history, had been up to that moment almost unknown to him. Deeply touched and attracted, Giordani put aside who he was and what he knew in order to go to the school of the cloister, desiring to begin to learn once more from the beginning.

In 1940 Italy entered the Second World War, and during this time secular disagreements between Christian nations became inflated. Yet, Giordani observed, an awareness of unity in Christ survived in the Octave of Prayer, which gathered together in peace the believers from antagonistic nations. The death of a young Trappistine who offered herself for the cause of reconciliation explains the nature of this unexpected coming together of Christians from around the world through their common resistance to war. Such reconciliation reveals that the Octave had nothing to do with either official agreements on

---

In 1925 they issued his essay "The Catholic Revolt." In 1935 he published *The Social Message of Jesus*, in which, relying on the teaching of the Gospel, the example of Christ, and patristic tradition, he affirmed the social mission of Christianity and the church; he was also engaged in relations between the Christian churches in *Crisi protestante e unità della Chiesa*, 1930, and *I protestanti alla conquista d'Italia*, 1931. In the following years he was active as an essayist, but he was also a narrator and poet. After World War II he was elected to the Constituent Assembly and the first Legislature; subsequently he remained aloof from political office and joined the Focolare Movement, of which he was a leading figure. During those years the figure of Gabriella was dear to him, so much so that she would be proposed among the ecumenical models for the Focolarini. He died in 1981, having spent his last years committed to ecumenism.

dogmas or with doctrinal synthesis: instead, it intended to redeem the tragedy of division, following the path followed by Christ on the cross. It was thus already a form of united Christianity, of realized ecumenism.

Thanks also to Giordani's foreword, the biography of Gabriella written by Giovanna Dore was immediately widely disseminated, occasioning five reprints at once; more followed in subsequent years. Exchanges between Grotta and members of the international ecumenical movements intensified. As a comfort in her mourning Mother Pia was happy to inform the mother of Gabriella,

> Listen, I have great news for you and for Father Meloni. From the 18th to the 25th of this month Dom Benedict, whose letters are in the biography of Sister Gabriella, was here. After wishing for so long to visit the grave of his little sister, he finally came. He is a holy man, but still an Anglican and full of strong and practical desires for reunion. . . . We invited some prelates here who are devoted to Sister M. Gabriella, and there was a most cordial rapport. A private audience with the Holy Father was held. They left moved and enthused. We hope that they will work even more effectively toward union and take steps to enter the Church with many others. Many want to come in, God willing![41]

Among those visiting Grotta were two religious who were profoundly influencing the ecumenical reality, Roger Schutz and Max Thurian, of the Taizé community.[42] Accompanying

---

[41] Gullini, *Lettere e scritti*, 114.

[42] Founder of the Taizé Community, Brother Roger was a theologian, the son of a Swiss Protestant pastor. In August 1940 he bought a large house in the semi-deserted village of Taizé in Burgundy in order to shelter war refugees. He maintained contacts with the pioneers of ecumenism, including Fr. Paul Couturier. Following the German occupation in 1942 he fled to Switzerland, where he met Max Thurian and founded the first nucleus of a community that began to draw students, workers, trade unionists, and intellectuals. In

them was the mother of Brother Roger, who continued to maintain correspondence with Mother Pia and to remain linked by deep friendship. Grotta was now a center for Christians of different confessions, the Italian home of ecumenism. This fact conferred on it the dangerous prestige of those who go against the current and condemnation from the resulting friction. Inevitably Mother Pia, in her openness to the separated brethren, was in the opinion of many beginning to become "impatient and reckless," as was noted by Ennio Francia, a priest who was considered to be her disciple.[43]

Among the first to misunderstand Mother Pia's role were the fathers of the Trappist Order, who became alarmed by the echoes of the biography of Gabriella and the turmoil that had been swirling around this Trappistine monastery. They began to consider this sort of conduct as incompatible with the strict reserve envisioned in the regulations of the Order. Added to this, another young nun originally from Sardinia, Michela Dui, also offered her life for the sanctification of priests; she became ill shortly after Gabriella and died of the same illness three months later, on July 23.[44] Inquiring about the succession of deaths—Mother Immacolata, Gabriella, and Michela—the monastic authorities decided to stop the work of Mother Pia, whose strong personality was considered to be influencing those events.

1944 he returned to Taizé with some companions. In 1949 he professed the first seven brothers. The Rule of Taizé concludes, "Do not ever participate in the scandal of the separation of Christians, who all so easily profess 'love your neighbor,' but remain divided. Have a passion for the unity of the body of Christ" (Roger Schutz, *The Rule of Taizé* [Taizé: Les Presses de Taizé, 1968]). The community is made up of members of different churches, Reformed, Lutherans, Anglicans, and Roman Catholics, promoting missions in every part of the world.

[43] Gullini, *Lettere e scritti*, 32.

[44] Tonino Cabizzosu, "Una vita spesa per la santificazione del clero," *L'Osservatore Romano*, 2 March 2005; and Tonino Cabizzosu, *Maria Michela Dui, una trappista barbaricina vittima per i sacerdoti* (Cagliari: Grafiche Ghiani, 2005).

The gap that opened up between this female community and the abbots who cared for it is partly understandable; the early 1940s were still far from having reached today's understanding that monasticism is a natural breeding ground for ecumenism. The reason for this reality lies in the earliest origins of monasticism, when some devout Christians felt the imperative to preserve the spirit of the primitive church, in which believers lived as one in heart and soul (Acts 4:32). These were the first *monazontes* (Greek, "those living alone"), leaving their cities in the Middle East and going into the desert to devote themselves to the search for God, committing themselves to fully translate the gospels into everyday life. In this spiritual culture, therefore, the lives of Christians implied an immediate proximity to the person of Christ, in whom all denominations have their essence and so rediscover the fire of Pentecost, descended from heaven on the disciples, to make all one.

Throughout history monasticism has continued to be a potential area of unity, even before the posing of the ecumenical question, because monasticism's primary effort has been to cultivate the Word of God, to live this spirituality in a simple, immediate way, and so to inspire others in their daily life.

Pierre Miquel, abbot of Ligugé from 1966–1990, explains this power of monasticism:

> Monasticism existed before the unfortunate division between theology and spirituality. Monastic spirituality is theological, and its theology is spiritual. It is spontaneously repugnant to monasticism to isolate a theological science that operates outside of a spiritual climate and a spiritual practice that develops outside of a theological structure. When a theology is no longer inspired by the Spirit, it soon becomes a polemic.[45]

---

[45] "Monachisme et oecuménisme," *Lettre de l'abbaye Saint-Martin Ligugé* 219, no. 3 (1983): 1. About the "ecumenical vocation" of monasticism, see Aldaberto Piovano and Maria Ignazia Angelini, "Il monachesimo come luogo di incontro ecumenico," *Ora et Labora* 58, nos. 1 and 2 (2003).

Monasticism has always been open to communication with the ancient wisdom of all peoples. In the course of the twentieth century the human sciences have highlighted the fact that the choice for monastic life is part of our anthropology, meaning that humanity has inscribed within itself the tendency to preserve for itself or for some of its members the opportunity to separate from normal social interactions so as to live in perpetual tension directed toward the divine. The monastic tradition of any one particular religion bears similarities to the monastic traditions of other religions, and it transmits these traditions. In other words, religious dialogue proceeds smoothly through monasticism. Where God is sought rather than defined, felt rather than studied, he makes people who are very different experience sensibilities that are similar.

In the twentieth century, Christian monks, streaming out from the ancient West to other continents and encountering different forms of asceticism, strengthened their identity after having been severely attacked by secular states during the nineteenth century. Universality was their nourishment, necessary for them to escape the anguish of the persecutions. Even Protestantism, which in its sixteenth-century birth described itself as averse to monasticism, in the twentieth century revised that original suspicion, noting that Christian denominations depleted of monastic life are easily compromised by temporal powers and lack the breadth that comes from being permanently open to the transcendent: contemplation.

Twentieth-century Christians noted that monasticism is for churches what the Amazon is for the planet. Just as in the jungle life reproduces itself outside of the control of human powers, so too contemplation is a zone of protected transmission, where the teaching of Christ results not in institutions, but in experience.

As a result of such growing insight, promising initiatives for the development of ecumenism developed, such as the foundation of Nashdom Abbey. Even Orthodox monasticism, which has various reservations regarding ecumenism, has acknowledged fundamental correspondences with Western mysticism by adopting some of its major authors, such as John of the Cross, Teresa of the Child Jesus, and Gertrude the Great of Helfta; on the other hand, Roman Catholics cannot help but find themselves reading Silouan of Mount Athos and Seraphim of Sarov.

Within the context of male monasticism, female monasticism in the West, especially in the more fruitful periods of its history, has lived in a state of empathy with the processes toward the unity of the church. An example is Hilda, princess of the Angles and the abbess of nuns and monks, who in her own monastery in Whitby in the seventh century undertook a project to join the usages and customs of Irish Christianity to the Roman practices. Then there were the nuns of the first Benedictine foundations in central Europe, whose wide-ranging experience of the glorious ascetic traditions of the northern Irish, together with the equally glorious traditions of southern Gaul, Italy, and the Middle East, promoted the convergence of these traditions.[46] For seven years the Cistercian Lutgard fasted to redeem the Albigensian heresy. Again, in the 1660s Mechtilde de Bar founded a religious order of women in Paris devoted to making reparation for the sacrileges committed during the wars between Catholics and Calvinists. Alone and without means, Bridget of Sweden fought a tough fight to recall the popes to Rome from captivity in Avignon, so that they would become the supra-national voice of all Christians rather than only of the French kings.

Gabriella, with the nuns of Grotta, is part of the same history. Unlike those who study its sources and catalogue its testimonies, these women are the ones who have radically lived this history. With Gabriella's offering, therefore, she

---

[46] Adalbert De Vogüé, preface to *Règles Monastiques au feminin: Dans la tradition de Benoît et Colomban*, ed. Lazare de Seilhac and M. Bernard Saïd, with M. Madeleine Braquet and Véronique Dupont, Collection Vie Monastique, no. 33 (Bégrolles-en-Mauges: Abbaye de Bellefontaine, 1996), 10.

performs the task that arose for monasticism in the middle of the twentieth century: to listen and witness to Christianity as the foundational reality throughout Europe.

And yet a fear prevailed among the fathers who had the pastoral care of Grottaferrata that it was attracting too much attention and creating a frenzied pace toward excessive autonomy.

The Exile of Mother Pia

In 1951, Mother Pia was deposed from her function in the abbey and assigned to a Swiss monastery, La Fille-Dieu at Romont, in the diocese of Freiburg. She left in the spring, without having had the opportunity to say goodbye to the nuns. Her career had so far been a parable: a novice at Laval, then nun, teacher, and finally abbess at Grotta. Moreover, she had extended her influence beyond the limits of the cloister over men who had considered her a spiritual teacher, from Benedict Ley to Ennio Francia, Igino Giordani, and even the editors of the magazine *Fides*, edited by the Pontifical Society for the Preservation of the Faith. However, now she was apparently defeated, and her "human honor," as she wrote, "was much compromised."[47]

Nevertheless, exile was an opportunity to get away from the role of administration and the goals that—regardless of the opinions of the major superiors—she could not ignore having achieved. Now she entrusted them to God, without worrying about them any further. It was a chance to go back to being a simple nun. She could also appreciate the opportunity to start all over again and renew herself as a subject or, better, as a cumbersome object whose disappearance might be a benefit for others:

> On my departure from Grotta I saw a chestnut tree being cut down in the cloister. I had often said to myself: "Lord,

---

[47] Gullini, *Lettere e scritti*, 80.

how will you take this huge tree away?" When the appropriate time came it was very simple. Brother Amabile climbed up on the trunk and cut off the large branches one by one; then it fell with another incision of the saw at the base, and then this big trunk, carried by some men, passed easily through a small door. . . . Really it was liberation! It bore no fruit; it only brought in humidity and cluttered everything terribly; those poor walls could not see the sun. I thought back to that chestnut tree when I left Grotta.[48]

Similarly, the writings that recount Mother Pia's leaving Grotta are very serene and gradually become even joyful. On her monastic name day, crossing the Swiss landscape, she noted, "the train runs along a large lake reflecting the marvelous color of the sky, and there is snow on the mountains. It is easy to abandon oneself to him."[49] Furthermore, she was convinced that the Trappist fathers, in cutting her off from her community, did so with good intentions, seeking the Lord. Even encountering her new monastic home was something positive, so much so that she was sure "to be so happy and satisfied as not to desire any other."[50]

It was comforting to be back at the beginning, with no more tribulation and responsibilities, an exile, a stranger among different peoples, "taken in by mercy." And it is precisely in the writings of this period that Mother Pia reminds us of Gabriella, even when Gabriella is not expressly named. Their nearly reciprocal roles were reversed now; in Mother Pia's happiness, she is satisfied with having nothing and in fact does nothing to try to feel better; the teacher is now the disciple of her former disciple:

> When one has already seen so many things, so many *bouleversements*, much doing and undoing of things that people had put their energy into, when whole lives, hopes, and

[48] Gullini, *Lettere e scritti*, 150.
[49] Gullini, *Lettere e scritti*, 53.
[50] Gullini, *Lettere e scritti*, 74.

ideals return to *vanitas vanitatum*, then one understands that God does not need anything or anyone, nor does he demand anything of his "little children" in their trials during their passage on earth: He only asks for love.[51]

During her exile, Mother Pia continued to be occupied with the biographies of Gabriella and their translations into different languages, as well as maintaining ecumenical contacts. In the meantime, the influx of postulants to Grottaferrata did not stop. Those who came there were young people who knew the biography of Gabriella or had read about her in magazines and wanted to enter her Trappistine monastery. Among other things, there were many people, not just the sisters but more often visitors to the church, and often the most skeptical visitors, who came to see the burial site of the "little sister," as she had been called by her companions in the dormitory of the sanatorium and as she came to be known throughout Italy as a result of the successive editions of her biography by Dore. Her tomb gave off an intense and persistent perfume, a prodigy frequently reported in the hagiography of every age around the graves of saints. Although the community, wishing to preserve itself from frivolous curiosity, played it down, the phenomenon continued to attract.

When the monastery at Grotta became too small to house the continuous arrival of newcomers, the nuns decided to build a monastery in the extensive countryside of Lazio, at Vitorchiano, not far from Viterbo. When they moved, in fact, they numbered eighty, and the buildings at Grottaferrata were insufficient to hold them.

In 1957 the bodies of twenty-eight nuns buried in the crypt of Grotta were exhumed in order to transport them to the village cemetery. Among these was Gabriella. Now, eighteen years after her death, there was an extraordinary discovery when they opened her coffin. Mother Pia wrote to a lay friend in a sober and cautious tone:

[51] Gullini, *Lettere e scritti*, 69.

> They opened the coffin of Sr. Maria Gabriella to find the body intact, mummified, despite the fact that over the zinc coffin there was water and the wood of the inner coffin and the clothes—everything—was wet. Present there was the bishop with the chancellor, the father abbot with two monks, the chaplain, two doctors, Rev. Mother, and four sisters. The seals of the bishop and the monastery were affixed.[52]

The event deeply struck the fathers of the Order who had attempted to control the events at Grotta by banishing its superior and limiting all forms of a spontaneous cult of the memory of Gabriella. This discovery made a forceful impression. The monastic literature of every era has noted the case of a consecrated person whose body was found incorrupt years after death, which later came to be interpreted as evidence of holiness. Similar findings are present in the legends of the martyrs and in medieval sources that tell of women who lived in chastity in monasteries or, sometimes, in marriage. Reading the letters that Boniface, evangelizer of Germany, directed to the religious of the ancient land of the Angles, we see how similar findings shook the feelings of the spectators, at times inspiring conversions.

Discovered in the middle of a century as disinclined to the miraculous as the twentieth, the intact body of the young virgin did not fail to evoke for the Trappist authorities the ancient *exempla*. In the same year, 1957, the general chapter of the Order authorized the opening of the cause of beatification, explicitly recognizing the great potential of the ecumenical witness of Gabriella. In February 1959 Mother Pia was recalled from Fille-Dieu to resume a position of responsibility in her own community, but when she returned to Italy she was suffering from a serious blood disease, in poor and incurable health. She soon died in Rome, on April 29, without being able to rejoin her spiritual daughters.

---

[52] Gullini, *Lettere e scritti*, 126.

Meanwhile, as most of the monasteries on the Italian peninsula have lamented the decline in vocations, the community at Vitorchiano continues to receive requests for admission. In the years that followed, several new monasteries issued from Vitorchiano: in 1968 the Trappistine monastery of Valserena, founded by twenty-four nuns in the hills of Volterra, and in the seventies and eighties the monasteries of Hinojo in Argentina, Quilvo in Chile, Humocaro in Venezuela, and Gedono in Indonesia. Then in the mid-nineties Vitorchiano founded Matutum in the Philippines, and in 2007 Naší Paní in the Czech Republic, in the diocese of Prague. In turn, these daughter houses founded other monastic communities: Valserena founded one monastery in Angola and another in Syria; Hinojo opened a house in Nicaragua; the Javanese Indonesian community helped form a Chinese community spontaneously created and then made a foundation in Macau, while Quilvo founded a community in Boa Vista, Brazil. In the Democratic Republic of the Congo, four sisters of Vitorchiano have pronounced their vow of stability at the Trappist monastery of Mvanda to collaborate in the growth of this new African community.[53] After this extraordinary diffusion had been consolidated, the young abbess of Valserena, Monica Della Volpe, gave a more positive understanding to all of this in order to settle questions that arose:

> Gabriella helps to show us the greatness of the feminine and contemplative face of the church. It is so necessary, so urgent to rediscover that face, because it is then that humanity can rediscover the lost part of our own face, of our own soul.[54]

---

[53] At the time of this publication, ten nuns of Vitorchiano have been chosen to begin a new monastic foundation in Portugal (translator's note).

[54] Conference at Vitorchiano by M. Della Volpe on April 22, 1999, Archives of Vitorchiano.

Introduction 41

✥ ✥ ✥ ✥

Reading the letters sent by Gabriella from the sanatorium and looking at her ravaged face in the photo taken during her last days, it is impossible not to feel a sudden rush of aversion. Even her two superiors, who had initiated her into the wisdom of the cross, were tried by it: Mother Tecla foresaw that she would lose the daughter in whom she had so much hope, and Mother Pia, hearing her cough, was tempted for a moment to contend with God. A young woman so simple and at the same time capable of embracing the absolute, so mature in spiritual learning, yet a child in enthusiasm: it was impossible not to hope that her candor wouldn't be extinguished, that her exquisite femininity wouldn't cease. We would have been tempted to distract her from the Calvary that awaited her.

It is the same awe we feel when we read the *Dark Night* of John of the Cross for the first time, in which he describes the pain of the soul gradually torn from the world and drawn by God: confusion, panic, loneliness, anxiety, loss of memory and all points of reference, regret, uninterrupted oppression and anguish, a sense of irremediable abandonment, alienation from the past, and loss of any future prospect. . . . One wonders whether in order for us to be transported to a higher level it is not really necessary to be uprooted from all existential foundations, whether indeed our flesh and its field of conflicts do not need such a resistance in order for an evolution of the spirit to take place. Is it enough for individuals of faith simply to have confidence in the vast capabilities given to them? Is it sufficient simply to affirm those living according to good morals and then try to keep far away from suffering, in the illusion—especially pursued in the twentieth century in which Gabriella gave her life—that good can prevail without encountering its opposite?

On the other hand, we also know from experience that it is only when we break all attachments to the ego that we can get closer to the meaning of our existence. Only by transcending ourselves can we be in touch with the depth of our own being. This is understood not only by consecrated religious and the saints but also by those who are not afraid to give of themselves. As any doctor worthy of the title knows, a person who has the talent to take care of his or her fellow human being, dedicating himself or herself with renunciation, does so even without reflecting that this talent lies in "the image and likeness" foreshadowed in Genesis. Artists know this when, intuiting in art the memory of Paradise lost, they exhaust themselves in carrying out their work. Likewise athletes, enduring the pain in their muscles, understand that the best of human destiny is to go beyond oneself. It is enough to read the biography of Madame Curie, written by her daughter Eva, to be convinced that to forget oneself is a life-giving blessing. As long as we are willing to stretch our limits for some worthwhile project, whatever it is, we all still have a high goal to aim for.

Even so, the ultimate sacrifice of a beautiful young woman in the shadows of a monastery might seem more impressive in the eyes of the world. Yet that sacrifice, which had the capacity to associate her with other generous souls, seems on the contrary to have isolated her in an agony, leaving her without any instant recognition, postponing the triumph that others obtain immediately—lives saved, works accomplished, or the initiation of a new scientific age—all for an inconceivable afterlife. The goal, in such a case, can seem so unattainable as to make one question its worth. Christian unity: think of the schism of the churches of the East in the eleventh century, the significance of which is lost in the labyrinth of the Christological disputes; the ninety-five theses of Luther, which caused the shattering of a continent; the Catholic-Huguenot wars that devastated seventeenth-century France; the harsh dynastic claims of Anglican autonomy; the anti-Semitism of Nazi Germany, which poisoned the Christian West until the climax occurred just as Gabriella was wasting away in the infirmary of Grotta. The civil and religious history we have inherited is so full of massacres, barricades, fires, trials, scaffolds, *auto-da-fé*, sacrileges, discrimination, persecutions, exiles, *lager*, and crematoria. Can the death of a young woman relieve the inflammation of such wounds, opened for centuries?

Gabriella certainly had not raised this issue. As she writes to Mother Pia, she only realized the greatness of God and made an offering of herself. To understand this it is not helpful to search for reasons; what is necessary is love. Unity is found in love. Igino Giordani, introducing the biography of Gabriella, claims to have learned from the nuns of Grotta that "one lingers at intermediate stations"—congresses, doctrines, assemblies of theological systems—but if one goes directly to the Father, one asks for unity by being united with him. The (theological) "prospects for convergence" that Paul Couturier had invited his correspondents to consider in 1938, the year of Gabriella's offering, were not possible for Gabriella's own interior sentiments, but they were realized nevertheless, because in love all divergences reunite. As Jean Leclercq observed, "she would not have been able to make any contribution to this cause, if she had not previously reached unity within herself."[55]

Loving Christ, loving him so much as not to be able to do anything other than identify with him: the meaning of Gabriella's story is all here. It is a story that the simplicity of her letters makes straightforward, so straightforward as to be understandable by anyone.

Moreover, the distressful pounding of a heart that wants to give life is known to us who live in the world, and we have attempted to do so, if perhaps only on an impulse. This is what a mother who has a dying child knows when she prays, "Lord, I have always been too proud; humble me from now on in every way possible, make my whole life a humiliation, but let this child live." It is like a wife in front of the body of her dead husband, when she wants to pass through the same death he

---

[55] Jean Leclercq, "Blessed Maria Gabriella Sagheddu: In Praise of Ordinariness," *Cistercian Studies Quarterly* 18, no. 3 (1983): 231–39.

did. To give of ourselves is fortunately within our spiritual capability. Gabriella was a lover who wanted to go to the same cross as her beloved. She is distinguished by her resolve to be happy and faithful throughout an agonizing year-long illness, to be grateful to the end, and to say, "I will never be sufficiently able to express my thanks."[56] Our own spiritual capacities survive, but the present moment distracts us from the faithful constancy and gratitude that Gabriella displayed until the end. Again, it was Monica Della Volpe who observed,

> The strength of this love, fully human, constructive, fruitful, and adept, in that small island limited by cultural horizons, was capable of a universal expansion. This is perhaps what is missing most today, the strength to accept the words "I want you for myself, and therefore I want you as you are, here, forever." Or even, "I want you for myself, and then, if you agree to give yourself to me, the horizons of your life will totally change. Belong to me; you are no longer your own. So your life is completely different now." This openness to the gift and this capacity to give is what we miss so much today, whether in the consecrated life or in marriage.[57]

Embracing a strenuous spiritual regime—roughly what Gabriella describes with modest words in the eighth letter of her correspondence, addressed to her mother—is what contemplatives have sought through the ages as do lovers in love: to adhere to the principle that rules the cosmos and unites it. Therefore they have frequently expanded their intuition to predict truths not yet apparent to the eyes of most of us. The nuns of Grotta had anticipated the impetus leading up to Vatican II, yet these same ideas, though affirmed by the Coun-

---

[56] Rosaria Spreafico, "'Non potrò mai ringraziare abbastanza . . .' : La Beata Maria Gabriella Sagheddu: un cammino ecumenico," *L'Osservatore Romano*, 21 April 2002.

[57] Della Volpe, *La strada*, 110.

cil, would take still more time to enter in detail into the collective consciousness:

> There can be no ecumenism worthy of the name without a change of heart. For it is from renewal of the inner life of our minds, from self-denial and an unstinted love that desires of unity take their rise and develop in a mature way. We should therefore pray to the Holy Spirit for the grace to be genuinely self-denying, humble, gentle in the service of others, and to have an attitude of brotherly generosity towards them. . . . This change of heart and holiness of life, along with public and private prayer for the unity of Christians, should be regarded as the soul of the whole ecumenical movement, and merits the name, "spiritual ecumenism."[58]

And so when John Paul II beatified Gabriella in January 1983, less than half a century after she died, the facts, people, and circumstances that had fostered her sacrifice were validated.

The ceremony was held at the end of the Octave of Prayer for Unity on January 25, in the abbey of St. Paul Outside the Walls, in the presence of representatives of the various Christian churches and ecumenical centers such as Taizé and Nashdom. In his homily, based on the contents of the readings of that day—Paul's conversion and his participation in the passion of Christ—the pope noted the correspondence of those acts with the life of Gabriella. This correspondence consists especially in the personal relationship that Gabriella had with her Lord, to which she gave priority over all else. Because of this she could give to an earthly consideration, that is, to the separation of believers, an otherworldly response:

---

[58] *Unitatis redintegratio*, chaps. 2, 7–8; http://www.vatican.va/archive/hist_councils/ii_vatican_council/documents/vat-ii_decree_19641121_unitatis-redintegratio_en.html.

It is the discovery of the Vertical, of the Absolute of God, that gives meaning and urgency and can make effective the horizontal opening to the world's problems. Here we have a cautious reminder, more precious today than ever, against the temptation of the horizontal Christian who is unencumbered by the quest for the Summit; a kind of psychology that ignores the mysterious presence and the unpredictable action of grace; of an activism that starts and ends only at the earthly level and perspective; of a brotherhood that denies the light of a common Divine Fatherhood. It is from this premise that the heroic gesture of Sister Maria Gabriella rises to the heights of a great ecclesial event.[59]

In fact, beyond her official recognition, if when reading her letters we discover that Gabriella is a person who has become dear to us, that is because it is also for our benefit that she reached that point in life where God is God.

Mariella Carpinello
Rome, May 7, 2006—Good Shepherd Sunday[60]

---

[59] John Paul II's entire homily appears in Quattrocchi, *La Beata Maria*, 275. For a recent commemoration of the beatification, see Augusta Tescari, "La Beata Maria Gabriella Sagheddu a vent'anni dalla beatificazione," *Vita Nostra* 33, no. 1 (2004).

[60] I wish to thank Augusta Tescari and Maria Paola Santachiara, nuns of Vitorchiano, for their support and cooperation.

The Letters of Blessed Gabriella[1]

1. To her Mother

Grottaferrata, October 2, 1935

Dearest Mamma,

With great pleasure I write to you to let you know that I arrived at my destination. I have been here since Monday at noon, but I am outside [the enclosure][2] for a few days, perhaps until the end of the week. The trip went very well in the car as well as in the train and the steamer.

Gavina[3] was so kind to me in Rome; she showed me many churches and took me to climb the Scala Santa, and so I send you this little picture that I took there as a remembrance. She also took me to St. Mary Major and St. John Lateran, very beautiful churches, but the church of St. Praxedes is also beautiful, where one sees the column to which Jesus was tied during the scourging.

And how are you all? Is the time of sorrow past? I hope so, because you have to resign yourself and instead be happy,

---

[1] This translation is based on the Italian text: *Lettere dalla Trappa*, ed. Mariella Carpinello (Milan: Edizioni San Paolo, 2006). That text respected the spelling of the original text, even when incorrect, with slightly modified punctuation. This translation prints letters by M. Pia Gullini and her ecumenical correspondents in italics to distinguish them from Sr. Gabriella's letters.

[2] On arrival Maria was received in the guesthouse. She entered the monastic enclosure five days later.

[3] The woman who accompanied Maria during the ferry trip from Dorgali and hosted her in Rome.

thinking that it is a great grace that the Lord gave me, for which I was unworthy. Thank God, I am fine, and I want you to know that they have dressed me as a *signorina*.[4] I spoke with the Reverend Mother Superior, and she told me that Sunday will be the ceremony of reception of the habit for Sister Rosa, that is, Maddalena. Remember to pray for her and for me on that day, because we need it.[5]

If you knew how good the Reverend Superior is! She seems more a heavenly mother than an earthly one. That's how good her advice and her words are, and the Novice Mistress, with whom I've spoken today, is also very good.

If you heard the choir sisters sing you would say it seems like a great number of angels and not people.

Everything here inspires peace and quiet in me, and I hope, with the help of the Lord, to be just fine; I'll write again when I go into the enclosure.

My affection I leave with you all, my brother, sister, and brother-in-law; say hello to all the relatives and neighbors, Grandma Francesca, and Grandma Michela, and let me know if she is healed and if she had the operation.

Greetings to Maria Fancello, Anna Pateri, Michelangela, and Mallena Lai, and tell Maria to greet the president[6] and the sisters of Giuseppedda's circle. Finally, warmest regards to you all, because if I were to write the names of everyone there wouldn't be enough paper.

I kiss your hands and ask you to bless me.

> Your daughter,
> Maria Sagheddu

---

[4] Maria arrived at the monastery in her traditional Dorgali dress; she was now wearing the black dress of the postulants.

[5] Maddalena Fancello, one of the young women of Dorgali, entered the Trappist monastery of Grottaferrata on the advice of Father Meloni.

[6] The president of the Young Women's circle of Catholic Action, Caterina Anna Secci Gisella.

2. To her Mother

Grottaferrata, October 7, 1935
Praised be Jesus Christ

Dearest Mamma,

The other day I wrote you a letter to let you know of my arrival, and now I am writing this note in order to send it in Sister Rosa's letter. My health is fine, and I hope that so is yours and the family's.

I want you to know that Saturday night I entered the community, and yesterday, the day of Our Lady of the Rosary, is the first day I spent in the Lord's house. Yesterday the clothing ceremony of Sister Rosa and the profession of Sister Michela took place.[7]

It was so beautiful and at the same time moving to see the two young women kneeling and waiting, one dressed in white and wearing a crown of roses, receiving a blessing for herself and for the new habit she was going to wear, and the other who in front of all declared herself to be the faithful spouse of Jesus Christ for life.

Pray, Mother, that this day will come for me too, that I will not have come here to see the sights but to remain always as a faithful spouse of Jesus. Don't think that now that I'm in the enclosure everything that you always heard about it is true, as, for example, that the food and drink of the sisters comes to each one through a turnstyle in the wall; no, we are very well in the refectory and we all eat together.

As for the place, it is a true paradise on earth. When I went out for a walk yesterday I saw the grapevines, which are a marvel, because they are still full of grapes; I also saw the vegetables, cabbage, fennel, and, in short, everything that can be in a vegetable garden. Today I took a walk in the garden and saw the few flowers that are still there now, but there are

---

[7] Michela Dui, who offered her life for the sanctification of priests and died of tuberculosis on July 23, 1939.

also flower beds for the flowers of other seasons, and there's a beautiful statue of St. Joseph with baby Jesus that stands out among the green ivy.

Enough for today, the rest I'll tell you another time. Let me know if Salvatore is back and how he is, and if he was on time to get to the car.[8] My affectionate regards to you and all the family; say hello to all the neighbors and acquaintances, aunts, and cousins, and Grandma Michela, and tell Maria to send my regards to all her companions. Once again, best wishes to all.

>Your daughter,
>Maria Sagheddu

Your daughter is fine; she is happy and has received the name Sister Maria Gabriella. Pray that she will be a saint and a blessing to her family. With religious sentiments,

>Sister Maria Pia, abbess

3. To her Mother

>Grottaferrata, October 17, 1935
>Sacred Heart of Jesus, help us who trust in you

Dearest Mamma,

The other day I received your letter and was glad to hear that you are all well. I too enjoy excellent health.

I have found many sisters here who are fond of me: I think there are more than fifty of us.

The day before entering the enclosure I met and spoke with Sister Margherita, who is very content, doing quite well now, and she sends her greetings to her relatives and to all.[9] On Sunday, that is, after the ceremony, I spoke with Sister Rosa. She is also happy to be here, and that day was even happier

---

[8] Maria Gabriella's brother.
[9] Originally from Dorgali.

for her, as you can imagine, because she wore the garments of the bride of Jesus. Don't think that I have forgotten you, for, as a matter of fact, I pray more to the Lord to grant you the graces that you require for your temporal and eternal life.

The last time I wrote, I forgot to tell you that my belongings arrived in Rome a few days after my arrival, but they were received at the Generalate of the Fathers, who weren't able to send them up here till today. But rest assured because, as I said, everything went very well.

The day I arrived here I seemed to be lost in a foreign place, but today that's not so; it doesn't seem as though I'm in the midst of people whom until twenty days ago I had never seen; instead I feel as if I am among people among whom I was born, lived, and grew up with.

It's so beautiful to live in the house of the Lord. The hours of prayer are fixed, and so is the time for work, so that no one goes around according to her whim, and only in the moments of each interval can one read or write, or go to the church as she wishes. As to the hour of rising, the novices and professed rise at 2:00 a.m., but I and some other postulants who are still in their first month here get up at four.

The work can be in the vineyard, the vegetable garden, or also in the community. The silence, I tell you, is such a beautiful thing because this way we don't criticize or murmur as in our hometown, but each goes about her business and does not think of anything else.

If you saw the sisters speaking with the signs[10] you'd certainly laugh and say, "Oh! So many deaf mutes!" Mute, yes, but willingly, for God's sake. Sometimes I laugh when I speak, because I still don't know all the signs, and I don't always understand. Ask the Lord to help me not only to understand what they say to me, but also to put the teachings into practice, that is, to obey the superiors and to observe exactly the rule of my Institute [Order], and so become holy before God.

---

[10] That is, Cistercian hand signs.

As for my name, I hope you will like it: it's the beautiful name of the Archangel Gabriel, whom the Lord chose to announce to Mary that great event.

In Jesus, I'll finish now with my greetings to all of you, my brother, sister, brother-in-law, and children. Regards to the family of Aunt Daddai and all the other aunts and relatives, neighbors, and acquaintances and everyone who asks for me. I hope that Grandma Michela is healed, and tell her that I have already prayed that the Lord will hear her.

> Your daughter,
> Sister Gabriella

Greet Mr. Muceli and his family, and, when he writes, send them my regards.

4. To Father Basilio Meloni

Grottaferrata, December 1935

Very Reverend Father,

The other day Reverend Mother gave me news of you, and I was very happy. She gave me permission to write sooner, but I didn't have time. Reverend Mother told me that you were transferred to Ollolai, and so I think that my village will have to resign itself to its loss. In this, too, we must see the will of God. I wish you well in this new parish assignment; you can work among these people as you desire and gather abundant fruit from your labors.

These people will not be ungrateful, and I hope they will correspond generously to your loving care.

As for me I am fine in health and in every respect. Although our life is cloistered we can get fresh air whenever we want because we have a large estate.

The silence that is practiced here suits me, and I find it much better than mundane chatter.

We are fifty-four nuns. We do not speak except to Reverend Mother and to Mother Mistress, while with the others we use signs and a smile of greeting. Nevertheless, our needs can be expressed and we are satisfied.

There is some opposition within me, but I think this stems from pride and the contrast of my worldly spirit to the religious spirit that reigns in the community, and I hope that with the Lord's help and by my conforming to the monastic usages, the difficulties will soon disappear. As for everything else, the satisfactions that one feels in the house of the Lord overcome the setbacks, not only the small ones, but even the greater ones.

The Lord is increasingly merciful to me, although I am unworthy and do not respond well to such goodness.

He wanted me closer to him because Reverend Mother placed me in the choir for the psalmody and to sing his praises. I should be very grateful and give thanks for this special grace accorded to me, but you can imagine, Reverend Father, how confusing it is for me, who never really understood music and singing. Nonetheless, I do everything possible to study it and hope that Jesus, if he really wants me, will help me.

For my happiness I must be grateful to you who worked so much for me, and I sincerely thank you. Indebted to you as I am, and not knowing how to express my gratitude, I always pray that the Lord will supply and reward you greatly, blessing all your undertakings and granting the graces you need.

I will never forget you, and I believe that I'm not hoping in vain when I trust in your prayers for me.

Please accept my sentiments of respect.

Kissing your hand I ask your paternal blessing.

Always your daughter in Jesus Christ,

 Sister Maria Gabriella Sagheddu

Santa Flora, December 4, 1935

✠ *Good Reverend Father,*

Thank you for your letter. If Sister Rosa and Sister Gabriella continue as they have begun, believe me, the Lord will be glorified and we will be very delighted. There is a true religious spirit in those two daughters, and that is the only important thing, although they are also very generous in everything. Sister Gabriella has a lot of trouble singing, but it is surmountable, I hope, with practice and effort. She is simple and serious and picks things up quickly.

As for Maria Fancello, I agree perfectly with your opinion.[11] Also, we are so full that for the moment the Superiors advise against receiving anyone else. The Lord knows what he is doing. It is beautiful to abandon ourselves to him with full and blind faith.

"Dominus tecum" in your new evangelical mission field. The One who sent you: "semper est mecum."[12] May you repeat that with Jesus, and add that onerous but precious "quia ego quae placita sunt ei facio semper."[13] And so we pray "ad invicem."[14] Sister Rosa has promised the Lord not to write or to read any more letters. Naturally obedience intervenes when necessary. She suffers the angel of Satan, but she fights well.

Best wishes for the approaching advent of Love. Bless me and believe in my deep appreciation and gratitude, in Jesus and Mary. Your very humble servant,

Sister Maria Pia

5. To her Mother

Grottaferrata, December 29, 1935
Praised be Jesus Christ who with his
precious blood has saved us all.

Dearest Mamma,

With this I want to give you the news that, thank God, I am enjoying excellent health. The Lord's house is a haven of peace and love, and I am doing fine here. I thank him always for

---

[11] A Magdalene Sister, known in religion as Sister Rosa.
[12] is always with me
[13] for I do always those things that please him
[14] for each other

having called me to himself and especially for having placed me in this house located far away from the world and its pitfalls.

You thank him, too, Mother, because I am not able to do it sufficiently, and pray always, so that he will quickly allow me to become a bride who is worthy of him, and tell him to make me suffer death a hundred times rather than leave these holy walls where I was greeted with so much love. I for my part do not fail to pray for you every day, and for all the family, for our relatives and benefactors, and, finally for our homeland and for the whole world.

Our mission is to pray always for friends and benefactors as well as enemies, and we will not fail to do so, hoping that the Lord will deign to answer our prayers.

Not having been able to write for Christmas, I do so for the New Year. As this new year begins, may the Lord fill you with his heavenly blessings and grant you and the others in the family the grace that you need for your temporal life and eternal salvation. Remember to call upon him, and he will certainly hear you.

Now I will let you know how we spent our Christmas. On Christmas Eve we go to bed at 5:00 p.m. I seem to hear you laugh and say, "too soon." We got up at 9:00 p.m. and we sang until eleven-thirty, but don't think that they were just carols: we were singing the psalms. Then at midnight we started the Mass of the Infant Jesus, also sung, and in this Mass Communion was distributed. Think about it, receiving the Lord before 1:00 a.m., and tell me if that doesn't seem better than having a feast with a lamb and roasted sausages as you do in Dorgali. After Mass we sang again and then went to take another little rest. In the morning we heard five more Masses.

Does it seem like too much? It was Christmas day, and we had to honor the Child Jesus who, for our sake, on this day deigned to descend from heaven to this miserable earth and lay in a manger in a stable. Let us meditate on this sublime lesson. He who is Almighty, Creator of heaven and earth, humbled himself so much, yet we, his miserable creatures, do not want to recognize our nothingness and our unworthiness. My dear ones, let us promise the Lord to recognize him, and at least from now on, to repair, as far as we can, the evil we have committed ourselves and all the sins that are committed in this world, which are very numerous.

And now, please let me know how you spent Christmas day. Let me know if you had the parish mission as expected and if it appears that Billia and Salvatore went to confession.[15] I would also like to know if the sodalities and religious participation of the faithful are going well and if our village has suffered considerably from the departure of Father Meloni.

As for me, I would like you to know everything about our life so that you'll have some idea, but you know that it's impossible to do it all at once, so I'll write a little at a time, and then you will be happier.

I send you this picture of the Queenship of Mary; Reverend Mother gave two of these to each of us. Pray these prayers so that soon this liturgical feast will be instituted.

My warmest regards to you all, Mamma, brother, sister, and family; say hello in my name to my neighbors and family, greet all my friends, and tell Maria Fancello to send my season's greetings to the *signorina* and all the sisters of our circle.

Happy New Year and greetings once again in Jesus.

    Your daughter,
    Sister Gabriella

Greetings to Grandma Michela and tell me if she is healed.

---

[15] Gabriella continued to worry about the spiritual life of her brother and brother-in-law. She did not stop asking for news about them at home until her last days.

6. To her Mother

Grottaferrata, March 29, 1936
Viva Jesus and Mary!

Dearest Mamma,

I received your letter a long time ago and was very happy to learn that you are all in good health, and I'm hoping that's how you are now. For my part, I am fine in both body and soul since I enjoy good health, and I thank the Lord for it.

As for the postcard you sent me at Christmas, I did receive it, and I thank you very much. I regret hearing that in our village religion has fared a bit poorly because of the departure of Father Meloni, but let us pray to the Lord and he will supply for everything.

Today I have the happiness to share with you some good news about myself.

It's news that fills my heart with joy, and I hope that it will do the same for you. The thirteenth of April, which is Easter Monday, will be the day that I receive the habit, the day that I have so much desired and waited for.

The day after the resurrection of the Lord I will become his bride. What joy, what happiness, what an immense grace to become the bride of God!

It sounds unbelievable, but it is true. What do you think, my dear ones, of this incomparable gift? He, my Jesus, could have chosen many other souls far more loving, more pure, innocent, more worthy. But no, he wanted to choose me, though I am unworthy.

My heavenly bridegroom granted me yet another grace. Reverend Mother placed me in the choir to sing his praises day and night, and this grace was given to me not just now, but from the first day that I entered the community.

I knew, however, that I am little adapted for singing, and that's why I have not written anything about it, not knowing how I was going to end up. This didn't happen because I can sing well, but Reverend Mother says that gradually with the help of the Lord I will learn. If you could see me sitting at the keyboard studying chant, you'd certainly laugh, and sometimes I get tired and end up laughing at my stupidity, but then I think that it is Jesus who asks me to do it, so I give it another try.

My mother, after so many graces, so much love and so much partiality, how could I not dissolve in love for my bridegroom? I leave that for you to decide. On this day that will be the most memorable of my life, I still pray to my Jesus, that he grant me the grace to live as his true bride, only to love him and praise him; I pray for all of you that he will give you the graces necessary, within your state in life, for your eternal salvation and for all your temporal needs. I pray for the whole community and superiors, that he will grant holiness to us all within our state in life, and I pray for our relatives, benefactors, friends, and enemies, for the church, for sinners, and for the whole world, that he will grant to everyone the necessary graces according to our needs.

As a husband in the world does not deny anything to his bride and especially on their wedding day, so my Jesus, who will never be outdone in generosity, will not deny anything to me on that day. My wish is that you too pass this day in celebration and holy joy to thank the Lord for all these graces that have been given to me.

Go forward all of you to receive Holy Communion, even your little ones, and pray to God for me and ask for the grace of my perseverance so that, growing daily in his love, I'll perform all my duties so as to live in perfect submission of will to my Lord. Pray a special prayer that I may learn to sing well and thus correspond to this grace. I recommend that on that day you sing with me the Magnificat.

Tell Maria Fancello that I ask the sisters of the circle to pray for me, because I will have a special intention for the circle and for each one in particular.[16] That is enough for today.

---

[16] This *Circolo* was the youth club of Catholic Action.

I embrace you all in the Heart of Jesus. Greet all the neighbors, relatives, and acquaintances, and greet the family of Sister Rosa and Sister Margherita; we see each other all the time and they're doing just fine.

Kissing your hands I ask you to bless me.

> Your daughter,
> Sister Gabriella

7. To her Mother

> Grottaferrata, April 13, 1936
> *Viva Jesus and Mary!*

Dearest Mamma,

With Jesus I come to visit you and hug you all. Today was for me the great day I awaited and desired. I made the marriage covenant of eternal love with Jesus. He will be all mine, and I will be totally his own.

He, my creator, did not disdain to call me his bride. Although I am his miserable and unworthy creature who has never done anything other than not offend him, he has not rejected me, but welcomed me to his bosom. The love of Jesus is truly great, and no creature, however perfect, will ever be able to match this love. The love of Jesus purifies, burns, and inflames hearts.

I feel that he always loved me and loves me now even more. I understand the great predilection that he had for me to bestow upon me this grace, while he could have chosen many others more worthy than I who would have corresponded more generously to his love. But that was not the case. He wanted to make me the object of his mercies. When I think of this, I get confused at seeing the great love of Jesus for me, and my own ingratitude and lack of corresponding to his predilections. Now I understand well that saying that says that God does not want the death of the sinner but that he be converted and live, because I have experienced it in myself. He has made me like the prodigal son. Now I'll let you know about the ceremony of my clothing.

This morning at eight I left the enclosure and I went to the part of the church where we don't usually enter. Now you must know that our church is like St. Mary Magdalene's, even a little smaller. In the place where there's a balustrade at the Magdalene, here we have a grate. This is a wooden structure woven so that the holes do not have more than the width of four or five fingers. For Mass and Benediction it's open, but after the services it is closed from our side with a black canvas.

In the middle of the grate there is a little door the width of two palms, and this is open to receive Communion. From the ground to a height of one meter there is also a low wall. We are on the inside part, and on the altar side are the fathers who say Mass. We have two fathers of our Order, the chaplain and sub-chaplain, who live in a dwelling attached to our monastery, but outside the cloister. They both say Mass every day.

Now you should know that the ceremony for the lay sisters is done inside, but I, being a choir nun, had to pass to the altar side. Thus at eight o'clock the Solemn Mass began, said by Father Abbot, who came for the ceremony, because these Masses must be celebrated by him alone. When the Mass was finished he preached a sermon all for me as is customary.

If you could have heard it, Mamma and all of you, you certainly would have been moved by everything he said to me in such beautiful and sublime words. He told me about Jesus, his love, my happiness, my blessedness at being welcomed into his home as his bride.

Since I knew that you'd like it, I intended to send you what he wrote, but the Father Abbot had to leave right away, so I was not able to get it. If I do, I will send it to you the next time I write to you.

After the sermon the habits were blessed. Then I presented myself on my knees before Father Abbot, who gave me a lighted candle as a symbol of the inner light and the crucifix as a symbol of faith.

After that the *Veni Creator* was intoned, and at the end of the first verse we went out in procession. Father Abbot and two fathers went ahead, and then I went with a young woman at my side who had to accompany me and carry my candle, and behind us there were some religious brothers and many women who always come to these ceremonies. I was dressed in a white silk dress and a veil that went down to the feet, just as at times you might have seen on some of the young women when they get married in Dorgali. In the manner I've described we arrived at the door of the cloister, where I waited for the community.

At the door was Reverend Mother, who asked me what I was seeking. I had to answer, "the mercy of God and of the Order." Then the Father Abbot said a few words recommending me to Reverend Mother. After that she took me by the hand, according to the usages of our order, and we went in procession to the church. Reverend Mother took the silk dress, and I put on a wool one, which is what I must always wear. This is also white, because the choir nuns dress this way. They put the scapular on me, which is a strip of white wool the width of a palm and a half down the front and on the back, three fingers shorter than the habit.

Over the habit and scapular came a band of the same white wool and a cloak that falls to my feet, just like that of Saint Therese of the Child Jesus. On my head five strands of hair were cut in the form of a cross.

They put a white cotton veil, a front piece, and the wimple on me. Until yesterday, and indeed until this morning, I was dressed all in black, with a dress, veil, and small mantle that went down to my elbows. From now on I will dress all in white. Before this if I had been seen in Dorgali, they would have called me a little widow, but now they would say I was a member of the Confraternity of the Holy Cross. After I was clothed as a nun, Father recited some other prayers, and at the end the *Te Deum* was sung.

During this hymn, I was led by the mistress [of novices] to embrace all the professed choir religious. Before this, however,

I was given a crown of roses by Reverend Mother while singing the *Veni Sponsa Christi*. I have to wear this crown all day. When the ceremonies were finished and the grate was closed, everyone withdrew while I stayed to make a thanksgiving. You can imagine my joy, and I'm sure that you will also share in it.

I am sure that you indeed prayed for me as I prayed for you.

Always pray that I may be faithful to my duties and the rules, at all times doing the Lord's will and never offending him, and so live happily all my life in his house.

This evening I received your telegram, and I thank you so much. I hope that you had a happy Easter and that all is well. When you answer let me know how Salvatore and my brother-in-law are doing. I greet you and embrace you all in Jesus when I go to Communion. Greet my friends and companions, relatives and neighbors, and the relatives of Sister Rosa and Sister Margherita.

Please bless me.

>Your daughter,
>Sister Gabriella

I send you these memorial cards that Mother Mistress gave me. As you know, I neither paid for them, nor do I own them, so do what you think best with them.

8. To her Mother

>Grottaferrata, December 21, 1936
>Praised be Jesus Christ

Dearest Mamma,

Today I was allowed to write to you, and I do so with great pleasure. I received your letters, and I was glad to hear about you and to know that Marco Antonio made his first Communion.[17] As for me, I am in fine health and doing well in every

---

[17] A nephew of Gabriella's.

way. When Sister Raffaella and Sister Ursula came, they told me that you were disappointed because I haven't written for a long time. You are right, but forgive me, because I understood that we had to wait for the permission of Reverend Mother, but now they tell me that if I had asked I would have been allowed to write sometimes because I am a novice, but after profession, unless it is necessary, we do not write more than twice a year. So forgive me because it was not on account of any moodiness, and don't think that I have become insensitive to your love, because indeed my heart has suffered to think that I was causing you sorrow. But I offered it to Jesus, who suffered so much for us, and I hope that you have done the same. If the Lord gives us something to suffer for his sake we should be happy and accept it with gratitude. If we think of the sufferings of Jesus, from his birth in a stable in the rigor of winter and lying on prickly straw as we have been contemplating these days, his flight into Egypt, the harassment he suffered when preaching, and all the suffering of his passion to the point of shedding his blood for us, then what will our sufferings seem like?

So let us be encouraged to suffer if we want to enjoy the heavenly homeland. I do not ask the Lord to deliver me from suffering, but that he would give me the strength to suffer for his sake everything that it pleases him to send me, and so I wish the same for you.

Don't worry about me, because I'm doing just fine. We have an excellent superior, who takes such good care of us that not even a mother could do more. Tell my cousin Nanneddu Monni and his father that the year of trial they proposed for me is over, and that I haven't regretted it, because I am very happy. Nor would I change my place in the monastery—where I spade and hoe the ground, and do whatever else is needed—with what I might have if I were queen of the world.[18] I'd rather

---

[18] An uncle, the husband of Aunt Grace Cucca, hearing the news of her decision to enter a monastery, had commented that Gabriella would be exhausted by it within a year.

suffer any martyrdom than cross the threshold of my monastery. It's so nice to live in the house of the Lord and under the same roof with Jesus! The door of the novitiate from the church is the same distance as from your house to Michelangela's, but we don't go outside, because it is like a corridor.[19]

I promised you last time that I would tell you how we spend the day, and I will fulfill the promise. We all get up at two in the night except those who are not well or who do a lot of work, in which case the superiors may exempt them and allow them to rise at three or four o'clock. This is only for some, however, because the community can never miss the time fixed by the Rule. From 2:10 a.m. until 2:30 we have the Office of the Blessed Virgin Mary, and when this is finished, a half hour of meditation. Then we have the canonical Office that lasts from 3:00 a.m. to 4:00 a.m. At 4:20 a.m. we hear Mass and receive Communion. After Thanksgiving we recite the Office of Prime, and then we go to Chapter. About 6:00 a.m. we go to the dining room to take the *mixt* or, if it is a fast day, the *frustulum*.[20] At 6:30 we have the Office of Tierce and the second Mass. After three quarters of an hour's interval, in which we read—the novices also do some study—we recite the Office of Sext, which lasts fifteen minutes.

From 8:15 a.m. until 10:45 we go to work. After a short interval we have the Office of None, and lunch at 11:30. When we're finished, we can walk for half an hour if we worked in the house, and, if not, we can read, study, or go to the church. Sundays, Mondays, Wednesdays, and Fridays after the walk we have "repetition," which is an explanation by the Mistress on the Rule, the Usages, or other similar things.

From 1:30 p.m. until 3:45 we go back to work. Vespers begins at 4:15, and after a quarter of an hour of meditation we go to

---

[19] It was not necessary to go outdoors to go from the novitiate to the church.
[20] The *mixt* consisted of six ounces of bread, around 180 grams, and coffee and milk; for *frustulum* they had two ounces of bread, about sixty grams, and barley coffee.

dinner, or take the *collation*[21] when fasting. After another interval we have ten minutes of reading in common, and finally we go to church to recite the Office of Compline, after which we no longer speak even to the superiors. At 7:00 p.m. we go to bed. On Sunday, because we sing a part of the Night Office, we get up at 1:30 a.m., and on big feast days we get up at 1:00 a.m. because everything is sung. This schedule is for us choir nuns, because the lay sisters, who are not present for all the Offices, have more work and less interval time. It would seem that getting up at 2:00 a.m. would make a long day, but instead it seems we've just begun the day and already it's coming to an end.

Although I cannot speak or write frequently, I speak every day about you to Jesus in Holy Communion, and I ask him to come to comfort you for me. We are approaching Christmas Day and so also the end of the year. The Christ Child will come loaded with gifts to bring peace and love into hearts. Let us prepare ours so that we may welcome him willingly, and he will not fail to give us all the spiritual gifts we need. Pray for me, that I will soon become a holy religious, his bride in fact, and not only in name. I will pray for you during Communion, which we receive at midnight, and also during the Divine Office, because it will all be sung. I have been appointed to sing the *Gloria in excelsis Deo*. It will be a little out of tune, but patience; the Infant Jesus will accept it just the same.

To the old year let us give all our sins and our failures to be buried, and let us recommend ourselves to the new year, that it be a bearer of graces and blessings from the Lord.

I have not responded to you about the memorial cards for my clothing ceremony because the mistress told me that for the clothing of Sister Margherita they decided that only a few would be given to the family and no more, because not all novices persevere, and afterwards these things remain as a

---

[21] a light meal

scandal, and besides, the time is already past. When I make my profession, God willing, I will write, and then you can have them. Gavina, who had taken such good care of me, asked for one, but since there were only a few I did not respond to her, so she will have to wait for my profession.

We received the cheese you sent us with Sister Raffaella, and I thank you very much. I heard that Giovanna has a new baby.[22] I am happy and hope that the child will be her consolation and become a good servant of God.

Receive my best wishes for a happy Christmas and a happy New Year, which I extend to all of the family, relatives, and acquaintances. The Lord grant you a new year full of thanks and blessings, bodily health, and everything needed for your temporal life. I send my respects to all, in Jesus, and ask you to bless me.

> Your daughter,
> Sister Gabriella

9. To her Mother

> Grottaferrata, March 28, 1937
> *Viva Jesus and Mary!*

Dearest Mamma,

The Lord is risen. Alleluia! Alleluia! That's the song that we repeat on this day at every moment. Yes, let us rejoice in this solemn day of Easter that commemorates the resurrection of Jesus from death to life in order to redeem us from sin. During the short time of Lent we pondered the passion of our Lord, but now we meditate on his triumph. Our song on this day is totally inspired by this great event. I thought about counting the alleluias, but I stopped halfway because there are hundreds and I just don't have the head for it. Mamma, and all of you in the family, together with me I call on you this day to be

---

[22] Giovanna was Gabriella's sister.

firmly resolved to want to rise with Jesus, that is to rise from our slumber to a new life, holier and according to the will of God.

God's will is that we live purely, in the fulfillment of our duties: you, in perfect observance of the holy commandments, and I, in the observance of our Rule as well. Let us recommend ourselves to Jesus to help us in this difficult task of our sanctification, and he certainly will not deny his help.

I commend myself to your prayers because I, having received from the Lord more grace, have the duty to respond with a greater holiness of life.

For my part, I shall not fail to pray for you, as this is one of my greatest duties, and although I cannot write often, I commend you to Jesus during Communion, which, thanks to him, I have never missed except on the two Good Fridays. I'm sure he will speak to you much better than I could do myself by writing a few lines. I received your letter and the card that you wrote to me at Christmas, and I thank you very much.

I was glad to hear that you are all well. I was pleased to hear that even my godmother Michela has recovered a little of her vision. Let us thank the Lord to whom we owe everything, and so we will be worthy to receive from him even more grace.

As for news from me, I am fine. I enjoy the best of health because the air seems tailor made for me. As for my superiors, I could not wish for better ones. I live, eat, and sleep under the same roof with Jesus, and what more would anyone want in this miserable mortal life? My only desire is to love my God and my Bridegroom more and more, to become more and more worthy of him, and to become a saint. Do not think that I want to be a saint placed on the altars, which would be a presumption on my part, but I just want the sanctity of the perfect fulfillment of my duties.

When you write to me, give me news of your spiritual advancement. As for you, I'm certain that you will continue to receive Communion and hear Mass every day, but Giovanna, the children, and our men didn't write anything, so I don't know.

Tell me if Father Meloni is still in Ollolai. Ask Michelangela to tell me if she returned to Dorgali, if she takes Communion every day, and what she is thinking.[23] I leave you my warmest regards, together as a family, and I wish you a good and holy Easter. Greet our relatives and acquaintances. I embrace you in Jesus, imploring you to bless me.

  Your daughter,
  Sister Gabriella

Sister Gabriella is a good novice and promising.
 Sister Maria Pia

10. To Her Brother Salvatore

Dear Brother,

I had the idea to write these lines to give you news of myself and to wish you a happy Easter. Thanks to the Lord I'm fine, and I hope you are too. I wanted to know if you and Giomaria have made your Easter duty. Have you? I hope so.

I remember when you wrote to me last year you told me that you were not able to make it because you were in the country, and you can think about God wherever you are. You do well to think of the Lord wherever you are, but that's not enough. Tell me, brother, if you were a boyfriend and said to your girlfriend, "I love you but I cannot come to you because I have to be with the sheep, but I think of you where I am," what would she say to you? She would send you away and certainly tell you, "If you are always with the sheep and you never come to me it's a sign that you love them more than me, and you're not worthy of me." That is just the way God deals with us.

---

[23] A young woman from Dorgali, still in doubt whether or not to enter religious life. Later Gabriella will write personally.

If we turn our backs on him, he will do that to us. But if we love him and we go to him with all our heart, he certainly cannot be outdone in generosity, and he will greatly reward us beyond measure. My brother, if you haven't made your Easter duty yet, don't hesitate anymore, but run, and together with Giomaria go to Jesus, and he will enrich you with his gifts and benefits.

Best wishes and Happy Easter,

>Your sister,
>Sister Gabriella

11. To Father Basilio Meloni

>Grottaferrata, June 9, 1937

Reverend Father,

Reverend Mother gave me permission to write and give you some news about myself. I wrote twice at the time of my arrival, and I hope that you have received those letters. Things are going very well for me, and I hope it's the same for you. I enjoy good health and am very happy to be here in the house of the Lord.

If from time to time the thought goes through my mind that they could send me home, it so horrifies me that I flee just as if I saw a poisonous snake. At such a thought my heart feels itself failing, and I would be happier to be torn to pieces rather than to leave the monastery. My only regret is not to know how to love the Lord as I desire and as I should.

I feel that I am very tepid and indifferent, yet the Lord not only stands by me, but also fills me with his blessings. I received my religious habit on April thirteenth last year. The profession that with God's help I hope to make can't be made before finishing a year and a half more of the novitiate. I am a choir nun because Reverend Mother has wished it so, but I know little about singing, and I'm also very out of tune.

For that reason I wanted to go in the back[24] before my clothing ceremony, but Reverend Mother did not want that, saying that gradually I'll learn. I have to thank the Lord for all his benefits, but in a special way for giving me a religious vocation and bringing me here away from the world and its pitfalls.

I am truly fortunate to live in a religious order, because not only are we safe from many situations, but also, if unfortunately one of us falls, a hundred arms are ready to pick us up. However, I confess to having had a disillusion. For me to enter a convent and to become perfect was one and the same thing; instead I had to learn by experience that it is not so.

To reach perfection I have seen that we need to work and work hard, that even when entering the monastery I brought myself along with my defects, which urge me to fight continuously. But who cares? If perfection didn't cost anything it wouldn't be worth anything. The Lord who put me on this path will know how to rescue me in the fight to achieve victory. I'm very happy about my superior, and, in truth, I tell you, not only could I not find a better one, but neither do I wish to.

Reverend Father, I recommend myself to your prayers so that I may correspond to the grace of the Lord and worthily pronounce the holy vows.

Because it so happened that I'm writing at this time, I take the opportunity and give you my best wishes for your name day. May the Lord grant you a holy life, full of grace and blessings according to his desires, and may it be to the greater glory of God.

I always pray for you, because I owe you much gratitude for the concern you showed me, but on that day I will pray especially and offer my Communion for your intentions. Please accept my respectful regards and bless me.

> Your very devoted daughter in Christ,
> Sister Gabriella Sagheddu

---

[24] as a lay sister

✝ *Very Reverend Father,*

I can do nothing but thank you for the two daughters sent to me by God. Sister Gabriella is such a dear simple soul, humble, with a very versatile intelligence; she easily learns a great deal of what she is taught, and she is so pure in her thoughts and affections. I believe the Lord is very happy with her.

The Lord leads Sister Rosa in another way. She has an ardent character; she is impulsive and has had to fight a lot interiorly, supported by no ordinary grace. The mistress and I have had to pay attention, pray, scold, and inquire about things. However, so far it seems to us that she is truly directed by the Spirit of Jesus. Her docility and sincerity have saved her from temptations and pitfalls. She made her profession May 18, and her sister Maria, Sister Raffaella, took the holy habit! At home in Dorgali they had a party! And soon also their brother Zizeddu will enter the Franciscans. Zizza Mattu, now Sister Ursula, also came, led by a clear grace. She is happy, poor little child! and we are very happy with her. In July she will be clothed in the habit. Giovanna Boeddu, still a minor, is forbidden by her mother to enter; if Jesus wills it, he will make the way smooth.

Reverend Father, may the Lord repay you for what you did in Dorgali. Your friend, Father Pala, is your worthy successor. Vocations multiply. May Jesus help you always and be for you the center of your life. Bless me.

Sister Maria Pia

12. To her Mother

Grottaferrata, July 31
Viva Jesus and Mary!

Dearest Mamma,

I received your dear letter written after Easter. I was very happy with the news that you gave me and especially of your spiritual progress. I hear that you continue your daily Communion and that you go to Benediction every day, and, indeed,

I recommend that insofar as you are able, you do not abandon these practices. Even if at the time of prayer the Lord seems to turn a deaf ear, certainly the day will come when it will bear fruit.

You told me that Giovanna is more willing than before to go to church, but she can't attend because of the children. I understand very well that with five lively children she can't do whatever she wants because she can't leave them alone, but the Lord is so good that he is content with our good will alone when we cannot practice for legitimate reasons. When you can go, and don't neglect to do so out of indifference, then the Lord will not let your efforts go without compensating you. When you cannot offer to God what he desires, in his great goodness, he will accept it as if you actually went, and then, in order to make up for this deficiency, you can send the older children, and in this way you will show them the right way and turn them away from bad companions. Especially send Marc Antonio often so that when he has made a habit of it, as he grows up he won't avoid it. And my little Caterina, who was ashamed to make the sign of the cross, you tell me she studies the catechism competing by memory with the others.[25] I am happy, but why didn't she prepare for first Communion? At five and a half years of age, she certainly could. Please at least prepare her for my profession, which will take place after the two years of novitiate, and tell her to strive to study in order to please her godmother. You wrote me that Salvatore was not in the village. I waited in vain for his reply, and this made me sad because I guessed the reason for his silence: that he wouldn't do what I told him and therefore he has not responded. God willing I am wrong in this, but it makes me sad to think that I am in a Trappist monastery and my brothers, instead of getting closer to God, seem to want to turn away—I believe that the Lord is not very happy about

---

[25] A niece and goddaughter much loved by Gabriella.

that. I hope that Salvatore will return home now, and I'll write to him for my profession. For myself, I can assure you that I'm well, and the further on I go, the happier I am to be here. The Lord was really so good to me that I could not have hoped for better.

I know that my sisters in the monastery with me are equally happy, and although we can't speak, we love each other just the same. Always pray for me, because I need it, and I'll pray for you.

Best wishes, Mamma, brothers and sister, in the Heart of Jesus. Greet the relatives, friends, the family of Sister Rosa, and the others who are there. Please bless me.

> Your daughter,
> Sister Gabriella

13. To her Niece Giovannangela

My dear Niece,

In your mother's letter I found a few lines you wrote me, and I'm pleased about the news you gave me. You told me you were studying for the catechetical competition. Always study and be a real little Benjamin of the Heart of Jesus. Love the good Jesus very much, because he prefers the little ones, and go often to receive him in Communion. Don't be content only with going to Sunday Mass and Communion, but go the other days as well, because now you're so little and you can't help with your mother's work.

When you go to church take my little Caterina with you, so that she will also learn to love Jesus soon. Always be obedient to Mamma, Daddy, and Grandma because the virtue of obedience is what pleases Jesus. You asked for a picture as a remembrance. . . . I sent you the poem of the Child Jesus, and now since you asked, I'm sending you an image of Saint Joseph with the Child Jesus. Don't lose it, because I don't have a factory to be able to send these things often. Goodbye for now, and I pray that Jesus will bless you.

>Your aunt,
>Sister Gabriella

Pray very much to Jesus for me. Thank you.

14. To her Aunt, Cucca Grazia

>October 10, 1937
>Praised be Jesus Christ!

My dear Aunt,

Perhaps you expected that I would have written before, but I hope you didn't take it badly, because it was not due to negligence. Thank the Lord I'm feeling well, and I wish the same for you. With pleasure I can say that it's not only a year of proof that I give your husband,[26] but it has been two years, and not only do I not regret them, but I would willingly receive them back in order to live them again. The world knows only deceit, but Jesus is faithful to his word to give a hundredfold in this life, and in the future to give eternal life to those who abandon everything for his sake. I assure you that I have truly found my home and I could not have wished for a better one.

Consecrate one of your sons to the Lord in one of our Trappist monasteries of men in Italy; there are three, and you will see how much you will gain for yourselves and for him in eternal life and also for the present life. Meanwhile, I want to let you know that on the thirty-first I will pronounce my vows to devote myself entirely to Jesus. I look forward to the scent of the perfume of your prayers to offer to my Spouse while I pray for you. I say goodbye, because I don't know if I can write

---

[26] See note 18 (Letter 8).

any more. Receive my fond regards for yourself and all the family, young and old.

>Your niece,
>Sister Maria Gabriella.

15. To Michelangela Secci

>October 10, 1937
>Praised be Jesus Christ!

My dear Sister in Christ,

With great pleasure I write these lines to give you some news about myself. If only you knew how good the Lord is and how good it is to live in his house with him. The happiness that I enjoy in the monastery cannot be explained in words. On the thirty-first of the month I'll make my profession and become the bride of Jesus forever. And how are you doing? Haven't you decided yet? They wrote me that your father died, so then you will have no obstacle because your mamma was already content with your decision. Don't take much thought of material things instead; if your vocation moves forward, dispose your soul for the embrace of the Lord, and he will take care to provide whatever you are lacking. Do you go to Mass and Communion every day? Try not to miss it, and pray a lot that the Lord will make you know his will. If you do not have a good director, you should try to find one, because he will help you considerably to get to know the path that the Lord has marked out for you. Have great confidence in God, because he does not abandon those who hope in him for everything. Jesus made me feel the desire to write these lines so that they would console you. Pray for me, and I won't ever forget you. You always imitated me; do so even now and try to make a break with the world. I would like to take you today to Jesus. I wish you all the best in Jesus and Mary.

>Sister Gabriella

16. To her Aunt Giovanna Fancello Masuri

Grottaferrata, October 10, 1937
Praised be Jesus Christ!

Dear Aunt,

I write these lines to say adieu and to thank you for all you have done for me. I pray that the Lord will reward your generosity. I share with you that on the last Sunday of the month I will make my religious profession, and I ask you to join me in praying and thanking the Lord of graces for what he has done for me. Receive my farewell and give my warm greetings to your family.

Sister Maria Gabriella

17. To Michela Lai, her Confirmation Godmother

Grottaferrata, October 10, 1937
Praised be Jesus Christ!

Dear Godmother,

I write these lines to give you some news. Thank the Lord, I am always very well, because here everything breathes peace and tranquility. The walls of the house of God free me and protect me from the snares of the world. On the thirty-first of the month I will make my religious profession. I ask you and your family to join me in prayer on this solemn day. Receive my farewell because this is really my separation forever.

Affectionate regards to you and your whole family.

Your goddaughter,
Sister Maria Gabriella Sagheddu

18. To Anna Pateri[27]

When Jesus comes into your heart during Holy Communion, say a word to him for me, too.

Maria Sagheddu

19. To her Mother

Grottaferrata, October 10, 1937
Praised be Jesus Christ!

Dearest Mamma,

Thank you for the last letter you wrote to me, in which you gave me such good news. I'm glad you went to the baths, because in this way you will keep up your health and can always attend church. You told me that Caterina has already made her first Communion, and for that I am very happy indeed. As for me, I'm always doing just fine. I'll let you know the news that I hope will make you very happy as it fills me with joy. I was accepted for profession on the thirty-first, the feast of Christ the King. The King of heaven and earth, the God of the universe, wants to take for himself a bride as miserable and unworthy a creature as I am.

Yes I, a poor creature, will become queen because he wants it so. I could not have wished for a more beautiful feast for my consecration to the Lord.

You, my mother, must consider how fortunate you are that the Lord has deigned to choose a bride from your family. Thank him much for this predilection for you and this great gift that he has given to me. On this happy day, I ask you to double your prayers and celebrate as we do in the monastery, because this is truly the day of my marriage with Jesus and

---

[27] Written on a small picture of the Divine Master holding a chalice in his hand with the Host.

not like my clothing ceremony, because at that time I was free to leave and the community was free to send me away. I especially recommend that you not be saddened at the thought that my profession marks our separation forever. If you had been closer you would have been able to come to the ceremony or to visit me, because the visits of relatives are allowed twice a year, but since we are too far away you must resign yourself with the thought that this is the will of God.

Concerning the memorial cards, as I wrote you, I've been asked to request that you send me ten lire inside the envelope. I'll send them to you at the end of the month to distribute for the occasion. One is to be given to Gavina, as I promised her, one for the members of the youth group, one for Michelangela, and one for Cichedda. For me that is all that I have to suggest, but you know to whom you have to give them, and in fact, I recommend that you don't give out more than one at a time, leaving the others with nothing, because you know that there will be jealousies; hold on to your own and then do as you think best.

I ask the woman who writes for you to please re-read the letters before sending them, because sometimes I find things that are so incomprehensible that if I didn't have practice and guess what she wants to tell me, I would have a sore head like the last time, when instead of *Caterina*, she wrote *catena*.[28] I pray that whoever writes won't be offended by this, only that she'll try her best. Reverend Mother gave me permission to write some small notes to relatives, so please distribute those you'll find in your letter and in Salvatore's.

Apologize for me to those to whom I didn't write, because you know I can't write to all of them. Recommend me to their prayers and also to the members of the circle; tell them that I will pray for all of them. You, too, pray very much, and offer this sacrifice generously to the Lord. I'm sure that he will

---

[28] chain

reward you greatly not only in spiritual but also in material blessings and reward the fruit of your labors.

Warm regards to all in the Heart of Jesus, and from my heart I await your blessing.

> Your daughter,
> Sister Gabriella

20. To her sister Giovanna

My dear Sister,

I am very glad with the news that Mamma gives me about you and your children, but she says that your husband and Salvatore are always the same. We must have patience and pray a lot, and the Lord will certainly answer our prayers.

I thank you for taking care to send me a picture of Caterina when she made her first Communion. I want you to know that the thirty-first will be my religious profession, and I invite you to take part in my celebration in the union of prayer, with the children. I'm sure that all of you will go to Communion, and I especially ask the little ones to pray a lot for me, because Jesus loves children and listens to them.

Pray that the Lord will make me a saint and that I'll reach the heights of my calling. I will pray for you, and I hope that the blessing of Almighty God will descend on your family as well. I had prepared a picture for Caterina to remember her first Communion, but I think the letter is too heavy, so that will be for another time. I want the whole family to receive my farewell because my profession marks our separation forever.

I embrace you in the Heart of Jesus. Affectionately,

> Sister Maria Gabriella

21. To her brother Salvatore

Grottaferrata, October 10, 1937
Ave Maria

My dear Brother,

I write these lines to give you some news about myself. By the grace of the Lord, I am very well, just as I hope you are.

I wrote to you for Easter, and also to Giomaria, but got no answer. Why? I would like to know the reason.

As for me, I want to inform you that on the thirty-first of this month I will make my religious profession. I will be the bride of the Divine King, whose feast is celebrated on that day. My dear brother, you know that the bride and groom receive gifts, and so I expect a gift from you. What gift, you might ask me? Well, on this day I want you to return to Dorgali to celebrate, and go to Confession and Communion for me. Do not deny me this gift that means so much to me, and of which all the reward remains for you. I ask you also to persuade Giomaria to go with you; I didn't write to him because he doesn't know how to read. Don't tell me that you are not in the village, because I know that the feast of All Saints is an occasion for everyone to return home, but even if you can't, I tell you to do it another day. If you cannot go to Confession and Communion in Dorgali I'll be just as happy if you go at Orosei, because Jesus is always present in Dorgali as well as in Orosei or in Grottaferrata. My brother, bury the cursed human respect and fear of criticism that prevents you from drawing closer to the Lord.[29]

Today, if I had not paid attention to these things, would I be so happy, and the bride of Jesus? Never. Mamma wrote me that you're near Orosei, so if you want to, it will be easier to

---

[29] Salvatore was not practicing his faith and, moreover, thought that having a sister in a monastery was a kind of dishonor. Concerning this view, see Gabriele Fronteddu, "La Beata Maria Gabriella: Da social di Azione Cattolica a Beata per l'Unità dei cristiani," *Convegno Diocesano*, Dorgali, April 23, 2006.

go to Mass there on Sunday and to do as I told you. The blessing of the Lord will rest upon you if you observe his law, but if you despise it he will abandon you.

I await your answer, and not an empty one.

In parting, I assure you of all the affection of my heart, and I beg you to join me in prayer especially on that day.

Say hello for me also to Giomaria.

> Your sister,
> Sister Gabriella

22. To the President of the Catholic Action Club

> Praised be Jesus Christ!
> Grottaferrata, October 10, 1937

Dear Signorina,

I haven't written, and perhaps you and my sisters in the circle thought that I had forgotten you, but that is not so; it is because the monastery is a nest of souls who want to live with Jesus, and he removed me from the world in order to transplant me in his garden. These blessed walls protect us not only from the evil of the world, but also from its profane glances.

I wish to notify you and beg you to tell my sisters in Catholic Action that on the day of the feast of Christ the King, I will make my profession. I ask you and my sisters for a prayer, because if the Lord has given me the privilege of a vocation, he expects of me a greater response. I will pray for all of you as I sing the praises of the Lord seven times a day, and on the day of the profession I will recommend you all to Jesus. Let us keep united in prayer. We can hope to meet again one day in heaven.

I send you my greetings in the Heart of Jesus and ask you to send them to my dear sisters.

23. A Prayer written by her for her Profession

October 31, 1937
Feast of Christ the King

In the simplicity of my heart I joyfully offer you everything, O Lord. You deigned to call me to yourself, and I come to you with enthusiasm at your feet. You, in the day of your royal feast, wish to make this miserable creature a queen. I thank you with all the outpouring of my soul, and in pronouncing the holy vows I abandon myself entirely to you.

Grant, O Jesus, that I will always remain faithful to my promises and never take back what I give to you on this day. Come and reign in my soul as king of love.

I beg you to bless our monastery and to make it a garden of rest for your heart. Bless especially the superiors, who have major obligations before you.

Bless my whole family, and, in particular, I recommend to you my brother and my brother-in-law; make a breach in their hearts and enter there as king to take possession. Turn your benign gaze toward our whole Order, and make of it a breeding-ground of saints.

I implore you for your Church, for the supreme pontiff, and for our bishop.

I commend to your Divine Heart all my relatives, friends, and benefactors, my parish, and the association of which I was a part, that you will deign to give everyone peace, joy, and blessings. I recommend the benefactors of our monastery and the sister who had to leave, so that you will accomplish the awaited miracle.

I pray for the sisters here from my village that all may persevere in love. Especially I recommend Reverend Mother, the mistress, and my confessor, that you will reward them for what they do for me and give them light to lead me in the way you mark out for me, and grant me a great docility for obedience.

O Jesus, I offer myself to you in union with your sacrifice, and although I am unworthy and nothing, I hope strongly that the Divine Father will look with the eyes of kindness on my little offering, because I am united to you, and, what's more, I gave everything that was within my power.

O Jesus, consume me as a small host of Love for your glory and for the salvation of souls.

Eternal Father, show that on this day Your Son goes to the wedding[30] and will establish his reign in every heart, so that all will love him and serve him in accordance with your Divine Will.

Give me what I need to be a true bride of Christ. Amen.

    Sister Maria Gabriella

24. To her Mother

    Grottaferrata, November 2, 1937
    Heart of Jesus, may your kingdom come!

Dearest Mamma,

It is with great pleasure that I write these lines to give you some news about myself. According to plan, the day before yesterday I made my profession, and I am entirely consecrated to Jesus with religious vows.

The joy that I felt and still feel is indescribable. The world cannot give these joys and therefore cannot understand them either. Only Jesus can make souls experience these intimate joys that make them forget the sorrows of this exile on earth, and that light up more and more in the soul the desire for Paradise. These joys cannot be explained in words; only those who experience them know what they are. Before, I was always afraid that I would be sent away and that my desire to be all for Jesus would come to nothing, but now I am sure that I will always remain in the house of the Lord, and so my joy is

---

[30] On the special strength of this expression see M. Della Volpe, "A Model and a Guide along the Path of Ecumenism," *L'Osservatore Romano*, 17 January 2001.

immense. What joy, what happiness to have been admitted by Jesus to the mystical marriage.

The ceremony took place a little after eight o'clock, and it was not especially solemn, because that is done only for the reception of the habit and the perpetual profession, which will follow after three years. My veil and scapular have been changed from white to black, and the belt, instead of wool, is now of leather and comes down almost to the feet. The mantle was replaced by the cowl, which is a kind of dress without any form, with wide sleeves, as wide as the habit you see on the statue of Saint Maur in Dorgali—I've never seen anything else quite like it—only ours is white.

We had four Masses, two of which were presided over by abbots of our Order who are also bishops. After the ceremony there was a Solemn Mass with three priests, at which I received Holy Communion. In Dorgali have you ever seen a bride and groom, even among the rich and noble, who had a Mass as solemn as this at their wedding, with more than fifty people close to them praying, instead of people who go there in order to feast and get drunk? Yet I, the lowest of all, had this.

In addition, I was asked if I wanted to accept Jesus as my model and spouse, and I read the formula of profession, which I signed in the middle of the choir and to which I added a cross.

I made my promises in the presence of everyone, and I must keep the obligations that I have assumed. I am sure that all of you joined me in prayer, and in fact I urge you always to pray that I die rather than be lacking in even a single one of my duties.

Friday the parcel you sent us arrived, and I thank you very much. The sweets arrived very well and did not spoil. We found the raisins and dried figs from Godmother Michela; please say thanks for me. I received the cards from the aunts and my godmother, who asked my pardon for having spoken harsh words to me. Tell her to be calm because I don't at all remember her even having said such things. I received your telegram, whose nice words made me so happy, and I thank you all very much. Another telegram came from Grazia Lai from Naples, and since I do not know the address to write and thank her, I'm sending a note to you so that you'll see that it reaches her. If you haven't given away the religious images and if you still have some, please send them to me along with a memorial card because I don't have anything. I was going to take one as a remembrance, but the Novice Mistress sent them all out, believing that I had already taken mine. If you don't have any more, don't worry, I don't want you to give up the cards intended for the family. I'm glad to hear that the announcement of my profession was a source of joy for you and that you have generously offered this sacrifice to the Lord. I hope that Salvatore and Giomaria have fulfilled their duties—Giovanna has insisted that I pray for them—and I expect news from you about them.

You wrote that Caterina was sick with a fever, and I prayed that Jesus would cure her so that she could also participate in the joy of the family. On the day of the profession I prayed for everyone, and I am sure that Jesus did not look at my merits but, in his great kindness and generosity, filled you with graces and blessings.

Receive my warm greetings in the heart of Jesus, for you and all the family. Also greet all the relatives for me, especially Aunt Grazia Cucca and my Godmother Michela.

Pray always because Jesus never abandons those who turn to him.

>Your daughter,
>Sister Gabriella

Let me know if you have received the pictures, and I forgot to tell you that we received the ten lire.

I am sending you this picture of a saint of our Order, so that you will see how I am dressed: after work we put the cowl over this habit.

Good Mrs. Sagheddu,

Thank you for your letter and kind words and for the sweets that have made their appearance in our refectory. And thank you for your daughter who has given herself forever to the Lord, in whom he and we are very happy.

> The Lord bless you,
> Sister Maria Pia

25. To Father Basilio Meloni

> Grottaferrata, December 17, 1937

Reverend Father,

In due time I received the note you sent me in Reverend Mother's letter—thank you very much. I am writing these lines because I think I must give you some news that I'm sure will please you and that is such a consolation for me.

On October thirty-first I made my religious profession.

I could not have wished for a more beautiful day than the feast of Christ the King for my total consecration to him, who will become the King of my heart and my soul. My happiness is at its peak, because now it is not an illusion but the real truth that I have become the bride of Jesus, and I am certain to remain in his house forever. The vows are actually for three years, but I don't think about this, because they can't postpone [the perpetual profession] except for a lack of religious spirit or some dishonestly concealed disease.

Thank the Lord I don't have any disease, but I pray to God to let me die not once but a thousand times if necessary rather than be lacking in the spirit of my vocation.

I feel good in all respects. There is no shortage of interior trials, and indeed it would be foolish to think we can be exempt from them. I'm certainly not very proficient at performing the Office in choir, and indeed, in the early days every time I touched the books I cried because I just couldn't do anything, but now that's not the case. I make every effort that I possibly can, and then if the Lord wants to leave me in humiliation, may his will be done. I don't want to be sanctified except in love, in the observance of my duties and perfect abandonment to the will of God. He who brought me this far will support me in the future. I don't know if I will be able to write any more, but in any case, you will always remain in my memory, you who directed my first steps, for which I will always be grateful.

I wish you a Blessed Christmas. May the Infant Jesus bring gifts of holiness for you and for his people, and may he smooth out the obstacles that you wrote about that you found among your responsibilities.

I shall not forget to make offerings to the Lord for you, although my prayers are poor. Please accept this small spiritual bouquet that I offer for your intentions as a gift for the New Year: ten Communions, twenty Spiritual Communions, twenty Masses, twenty sacrifices, and ten rosaries.

I recommend myself to your prayers and ask you to please bless me.

> Always your daughter in Christ,
> Sister Gabriella Sagheddu

Very Reverend Father, I believe that Jesus is very happy with all your spiritual daughters. In union in Him,

> *Humbly,*
> *Sister Maria Pia*

26. To her Mother

> Grottaferrata, December 20, 1937
> Praised be Jesus Christ!

Dearest Mamma,

Several days ago I received your letter in which you gave me news of the family.

I was very glad to hear that on the day of my profession you were united with me in spirit, and went to Communion and prayed much for me. I thank you immensely, and I am sure that the Lord will reward you. You wrote that even Caterina was healed on that day, and I give thanks to Jesus because I prayed that he would do me this favor. I learned that Nenneda is sick, but hopefully by now she is healed. I waited in vain for an answer from Salvatore, who seems to be deaf to what I have written him. It is necessary that we make a commitment to pray for these men, and Jesus, who can even work miracles, will not fail to give us the desired grace. I started the fifteen Saturdays of the Madonna with this intention, and when it's finished, I'll begin again until we receive this grace.

I received the note from Aunt Grazia, who told me that I should not be offended by the words spoken by her husband. Please tell her for me not to even think that I'm offended by them; if she continues to think this way she would do me wrong, because I knew very well that they were spoken not to offend me but rather to test me. But even if I had really been offended, we cannot hold a grudge when we're in the house of the Lord; that is something absolutely contrary to our spirit.

If I remembered those words it is just to let you know that even if I had been undecided when I left, which was not the case, Jesus has made me firmer now more than ever in my vocation. We are close to Christmas, a feast so dear to our hearts, and it will be the third Christmas that I'll spend in the house of the Lord.

It is an ancient feast that always returns to us as something new. The Child Jesus in the manger will return again this year to remind us that it was for love of us that he became so small and in need of everything. In the eyes of those who live according to the world it seems a folly to think that the Almighty has been reduced to such a state for his creatures, yet the wisdom of all people united together is not worth a crumb of the infinite wisdom of God, who arranges all things reverently. May the Child God, who is full of gifts, come to you according to your needs, but most of all the spiritual ones.

When you go to his crib, the manger, that is, don't forget me, and tell him to make me spiritually little and in accord with his will. Being reborn with Jesus, in the new year, which will soon begin, let us try to live more devoutly in the love of God and in perfect fulfillment of our duties. I hope this new year will be full of grace and heavenly blessings for you according to your desires.

Since I speak to you for everyone, may this Christmas be for you and for all the family a holy day of peace and joy, of the peace that the Child Jesus came to bring into the world. In the Heart of Jesus, I embrace you, and I renew my holy wishes for you and the entire family, especially my aunts and my Godmother Michela. Please bless me, each of you.

> Your daughter,
> Sister Maria Gabriella

27. To Mother M. Pia Gullini [31]

April 19, 1938

Reverend Mother,

I write these words in order to give you some news about myself.

Yesterday just before noon, that is, immediately after the visit at the reception desk, I was taken here to this room in the hospital. The doctor visited me twice and did not tell me anything except to eat and to eat well. Tomorrow there will be a visit for X-rays.

Since I got out of the car, I have seen neither that young lady nor Sister Serafina, and I do not know where she is.[32]

---

[31] The first letter written by Gabriella from San Giovanni hospital in Rome after her offering. For the moment only Mother Pia, Mother Tecla, and Gabriella's confessor, Father Filippo Viola, were aware of the reason for her illness. A sister testified then: "No one knew the role that would be given to Sister Maria Gabriella. Everything passed between her and God" (*Positio super virtutibus*, 21).

[32] A nun from Grotta.

After the first visit to the office, while I was still in a hospital gown and cap, I was given another garment and told to go with the two nurses who came. I thought I'd be going to another room, and I followed, but I had to go through two or three outside corridors dressed that way.

Reverend Mother, I didn't look at anything, but imagine my confusion and my pain seeing myself exposed that way to everyone's eyes. When I got to the bed to which I had been assigned, raising my head, I saw in front of me a large crucifix. I stared at it and seeing that my Jesus was naked and that for my sake he was exposed to the public, I thought that my sacrifice was nothing in comparison with his.

My clothes were left at the entrance, and they didn't return them to me. . . .

Could you send me a white veil—they told me I could bring that—and also a lighter sweater, because the one I brought is very heavy, and it makes me perspire. Thank you. I hope to return after the visit for X-rays, and I earnestly entrust this to your prayers, in which I have much confidence.

I asked the doctor if I could return to the monastery, and he told me that after the X-rays, we'll see. If anything unfortunate comes up and I don't return, I'll let you know as soon as they tell me.

As for my soul, Reverend Mother, I'm like a fish out of water. I'm in a great big room full of people. Most of them are young, shouting, screaming, and making a hellish noise, and there is no means of being recollected for a minute. As soon as I arrived, they came close to me, and they wanted me to yell and make a racket with them.

Now propelled out of my solitude, I am in the midst of this world full of turmoil, and I feel the magnitude of the sacrifice. Even at night I hear coughing from left and right; some complain, others talk, and so on.

Sometimes, when I think of my monastery, and especially at night, the tears come down from my eyes, and I can't say anything other than these words: "My God, for your glory." And so I remain in peace.

The sisters don't come for anything except to dispense the meals. One of them accompanied me to the X-ray visit. I asked her for more paper, saying that I need to write. I do not know if she remembered, because she didn't bring me anything. I borrowed everything from a neighbor, so please send me some paper and some stamps.

I am here doing nothing. When it's necessary to speak, although I'd rather be silent, I do so in order to answer so many questions they ask me, in order not to be rude. I hear from other people that it's been a month for some, for others two, three, or ten months. For me, I think that instead of being healed I'll become worse if I stay here because everyone coughs and there isn't sufficient air. There is a small terrace, but I don't go out on it because it overlooks the road, and I am without a veil. I recommend myself again to your prayers.

I close for now, united with you in the Sacred Heart of Jesus. Greet the Mistress and all the others for me. I will pray for you in Holy Communion.

Sister Gabriella

28. To her Mother[33]

Grottaferrata, April 21, 1938
Praised be Jesus Christ!

Dearest Mamma,

I received your two letters and your postcard, and I thank you so much. Excuse me and forgive me for not having written before because it was certainly not due to indifference or malice, but only because I wasn't able to.

---

[33] This is the first letter Gabriella wrote to her mother after becoming ill. She did not mention the disease and did not want her mother to know that she was in the sanatorium; therefore she wrote "Grottaferrata" next to the date as shown in the letter, and she sent it in an envelope to the monastery, asking them to post it so that the origin of the letter would not be traced.

I was glad for the news about you that Sister Andrea brought to me when she came, and I thank the Lord for it. At Christmas you wrote me that Nannedda and uncle Delussu died. I felt a bit sorry, too, but we must resign ourselves to the will of God, and we must be ready to be separated from our loved ones if it pleases the Lord, and even ready to die ourselves, because we are never assured of a single day. You did well to write to me about that because then I could say the prayers as is my duty, and I can even say that you should write such things. Write also when you have need of prayer, because necessary things are always permitted, and never worry about writing useless things.

I hope that you all had a happy Easter, and I hope that you will rise with the Lord to an increasingly holy life. As for me, I cannot help but always bless God for welcoming me into his home, where I am filled with his loving care. Pray for me that I will glorify the Lord in the fulfillment of his divine will in whatever form it appears. After our profession we can only write twice a year, but do not be discouraged because in case of need, whether on your part or mine, the superiors can give permission. For you there is no rule, and therefore you can write when you wish.

I waited in vain for the answer from Salvatore, but it seems that he is not inclined at all and will not respond anymore. I don't know if he has made his Easter duty, but I hope that you have done everything possible to encourage him.

I always pray to the Lord that he may deign to touch the hearts of these men of ours who seem unwilling to bend their will to this great duty.

You pray too, because prayer disarms God and moves his divine heart to pity. If prayer isn't enough, I would even desire that the Lord make me suffer in order to obtain this grace.

My Easter wish is that the Lord would fill you with graces and blessings according to the desires of your heart.

I embrace you and send greetings to all in the heart of Jesus. Greet our relatives and friends.

I wish you all the best and I ask you to bless me.

Your daughter, Sister Maria Gabriella

29. To Mother M. Pia Gullini

April 24, 1938

Dearest Reverend Mother,

I promised to write you about the result of the visit to the X- rays. They were taken on Thursday, but the answer was given to me only yesterday. I don't understand anything. But if you want to consult the doctor[34] here is the text: "Radiological examination—condensation of all the upper lobes on the right lung showing a very white central area surrounded by smaller ones. An abnormal reinforcement at the base of the lung."

They won't let me leave here; actually they told me yesterday that I'll be here for a little while; now they say it will be longer. I cried so much that I cannot cry any more. I try to distract myself from this thought and calm down, but I cannot. My heart is torn, and without special help from heaven, my cross has become so heavy that I can no longer hold up.

Every morning they give me an intermuscular injection and every two days one in a vein in the arm. Today they gave me a pneumothorax, which is like an injection between the ribs under the armpit: by means of a certain device it introduces air around the lungs. It is painful, and I have felt it from this morning till this evening. Please excuse the handwriting, because I am in bed: they told me not to move because that could harm me. They injected four hundred centimeters of air.

I am in a hospital where there are not only bodily miseries but also spiritual ones. I hear things that I would never have been able to bear when I was in the world, so just imagine

---

[34] of the monastery

how it affects me now. Sometimes I turn my ears away and I cover my face, but I can't always do that. This life is for me a torment. . . .

Do as the Lord inspires you, but for the love of God, do everything possible so that I will soon return to the monastery, because I am convinced that the doctors exaggerate the seriousness of my illness. I am sending you a letter that I wrote to my mother, because if I send it from here, they would recognize the origin of the postmark. Don't tell them anything about my disease; otherwise in Dorgali they would say that those who enter the convent become consumptive. . . .

Thank you very much for all that you've written and sent. Yesterday and the day before yesterday Father Abbot came to see me.[35] Pray for me, because I have so much need of prayer. Sometimes I wonder if the Lord has not abandoned me; other times I think he tries those whom he loves, and yet at other times it seems impossible that God can be glorified by this sort of life, but I always end up abandoning myself to the divine will.

I greet you with all my heart, and I ask you to bless me.

30. To Mother M. Pia Gullini

April 28, 1938

Dearest and Reverend Mother,

Thank you for your letter and the prayers that you and the others offer for me. I feel their effect because these days are a bit quieter. Everything seems easy when we are at peace, but when the Lord tries us, we realize our weakness. I have offered myself entirely to my Jesus, and I do not take back my word. I am weak, it is true, but the Lord knows my frailty and the cause of my pain. He forgives me, and I am convinced of this.

---

[35] The abbot of the monastery of Frattocchie.

I received the rosaries and holy pictures you sent me, and I thank you with all my heart. All my companions in this room came around me, and in an instant the rosaries and pictures were gone because each wanted a remembrance of the "little sister" as they call me. They are lacking a bit in seriousness, but other than that they are all of good heart, and they love me. They would always like to see me laugh and joke with them, but I refrain because it's not my spirit.

After I distributed the rosaries, a nun saw one of them with the dark beads that she loved very much, and she asked me if we sell them. This is the sister who accompanies me to the visits and the pneumothorax treatments, so for this reason I ask you to send me one for her if you agree. Forgive me; I know I am demanding. They allowed me the wimple you sent me.

As for the cure, I wouldn't know what to say. I went for the pneumograph this past Sunday and Tuesday, and will have to do it again on the twenty-ninth. If I've cried it's certainly not been without reason, because I know that the cure is quite long and often causes many complications. I have no fever at all and no expectoration; the doctor wants me to expectorate, but I just cannot. I asked the sisters twice to give me the "cachet" for the phlegm, but so far I haven't received it.

Reverend Mother, I wish you a happy feast day and all that your heart desires.[36] I haven't been able to do anything for you, but I offer my prayers, my communions, and my sacrifices to the Lord for your intention to be sanctified more and more. He has permitted that this year I cannot participate in your feast day. *Fiat.*

I am doing everything that I have been told, and I eat plenty. I will heal if the Lord wishes it, and otherwise, his will be done. We will find ourselves this day in the Heart of Jesus.

---

[36] The feast day of Mother Pia was on April 30, the date of the liturgical memorial of Saint Pius V.

31. To Mother M. Pia Gullini

May 3, 1938

Dearest and Reverend Mother,

Yesterday the good Father Chaplain came to see me and brought me your dear letter. Thank you very much for what you have done for me, and please thank all the people who are concerned about me. May the Lord reward you all abundantly in heaven. I am very sorry that I displeased you with my letter. I don't want to apologize so many times, but only ask forgiveness with all my heart.

Last Sunday, as I told Father, they examined my sputum and it was found positive. I had placed all my hope in this exam, so you understand what pain this news has caused me.

The first day I suffered very much. Then, last night, I felt a great strength infused into my heart, and I resigned myself fully to the will of God, accepting to suffer for his glory and not to endanger my sisters.

I assure you that my sacrifice is entirely complete, because from dawn until late at night I don't do anything except totally renounce my will, my aspirations, my desires, and everything that is in me, whether holy or defective.[37]

Previously there was no way to bend my heart; now I truly understand that the glory of God and being a victim does not mean to do great things; rather it consists in the total sacrifice of oneself. Pray for me, that I will increasingly understand the great gift of the cross and that from now on it will benefit me and all the others.

I feel that now you love me more and that also my heart increases in my love for you. In this regard I suffered a lot both from the devil, who tempted me to judge my superiors as heartless for leaving me here, and also from other people who

---

[37] The invitation for the Octave of Prayer of Paul Couturier of January 1938 reads, among other things, "The prayer of a Christian is so much more effective for union when the person is close to God that is, stripped of self."

make the same accusation. I certainly did not hesitate to drive out these temptations, and I assure you that I won. I say this with filial simplicity, and if I could show you my heart like an open book, I would be happy to do so.

The Lord keeps me naked on the cross, and I have no other consolation than to know that I suffer in order to fulfill God's will in a spirit of obedience.

It seems at times that my head is so confused: when I start the rosary I go on to say the chaplet of mercy. I begin that, and then I find myself doing prayers for the dead, and so on, and then I say with the psalmist, "I was like a beast before you. Nevertheless I am continually with you."

Today I inform you that they will take me to the section of the hospital where Sister Serafina is, but I don't know yet if they will keep me with her. I didn't want to go there, because the Reverend Father Abbot and Father Chaplain told me that I should have gone somewhere else, and that this change was not necessary, but the order came, and I just submitted. As you see, for the moment the Lord does not give you the consolation of my return, nor do I know if he will give me the grace to return to the monastery.

If you agree, please send me at least the breviary, because they haven't given me any work; so by saying the Office I'll spend the time more piously. I don't need anything else now. If I am going to be transferred elsewhere, I'll let you know what I need.

Reverend Mother, you asked me to pray for you during these days. You may be sure that I do, because my only consolation is to pray as well as I can. I could not finish this letter in the common room, so I do it in another wing of the sanatorium.

I was put in a small room with a Franciscan nun who seems very good. Here I am much better than in the common room, and I thank the Lord for this. I do not know if it will be convenient to change my room again, but as the Lord gives you the grace to see further than I can, Reverend Mother, do what you think is best.

I feel certain that gradually as the result of resignation, a great peace enters me. . . . Tomorrow and the day after I will offer my day for you, praying to the Lord to bless and sanctify you more and more so that you can sanctify the others. I commend myself to your prayers, in which I put all my hope.

I greet you with the most filial affection, and I embrace you wholeheartedly.

>Your daughter,
>Sister Maria Gabriella

Bless me. . . . The leaflets that you sent me have done good to those who read them in the common room. I hope that the effect lasts!

32. To Mother M. Pia Gullini

May 10, 1938

Dearest Reverend Mother,

Yesterday I received your package and your letter and I thank you for everything. I understand your decision about my return; I know you do everything for my greater good, but I don't hide the fact that this was painful for me. If I had been told eight days ago that I had to stay here for the cure, I would have been resigned, and it wouldn't have bothered me so much. But after Father Abbot told me and repeated again on Saturday that I could return to the monastery this week, I felt invaded by a great joy; therefore this shock was terribly hard for me, because I am in a state of great physical weakness.

The wound[38] has reopened and bleeds again as at the beginning, and it has made a deep furrow in my heart. Be patient! I tell myself. The Lord also gave me this test to add to the others that will follow, because I am sure that this will not be the only one. If he wishes it, after the first moment of anguish, every-

---

[38] *morale*: Italian ed.

thing will come back in place as before, and his will shall be fulfilled.

When I left, Reverend Mother, you said that if I had to stay, it would be at most for a few weeks; but it's been a month, and who knows how long I'll still be here. I hope at least you don't have the intention of keeping me out too long.

Now that I am back in the midst of the world, I feel more than ever the greatness of the gift of a vocation, especially for our way of life and how we must make the most of it. Pray for me: when you are used to living the Trappist spirituality it demands a great resignation and great faith to endure a life extremely contrary to ours and full of moral humiliation. For consecrated souls it is very painful to be at the mercy of everyone.

The doctor is full of respect for me, but that does not detract from my repugnance. I am always afraid of losing my religious spirit. So I stay here and do not leave my room except to go to church. Some tell me I'm too reserved, that I should relax while being out of the monastery. I don't mind what they say, but I feel that if I were to do that, my spirit would feel more pain instead of being lifted up. Nothing can give me relief, except the thought of doing the will of God and obedience to the superiors.

Concerning the religious sister who is with me, she is very good, and we get along because she also has a tendency to solitude. Sometimes our ideas do not agree, but we do fine just the same. . . . She is absolutely against my leaving here, saying that if it is the will of the superiors, I must do what they say, and so I should not wish to return to the monastery without having finished the treatment, because in the monastery I could not have the injections and special meals as in the hospital. To all this I replied that I would be much happier to live closed up in a well in the monastery than live here with all the care and comfort desirable. . . .

We go to bed at nine, but for eight days I have woken up at one or two o'clock: a sore throat and cough impede my breathing and prevent me from sleeping. During the day I go to bed, but I don't sleep; for two or three days the food has nauseated me, and I also have a fever.

Always your daughter, who only wants to return to your embrace,

> Sister Maria Gabriella

I profited from *The Imitation of Christ* chapter 37 of Book III.[39]

33. To Mother M. Pia Gullini

Sunday, May 22, 1938

Dearest Reverend Mother,

Thank you very much for your dear letter and for what you sent me, which I received this morning. Thank you for your good words and good advice.

For a long time I have been convinced that I am only a pygmy in the way of the spirit, because I get carried about with every wind that blows. My soul is here like one lost, because it doesn't have its mother[40] or a friend whom it can ask for advice when it feels the need. It seems to me that the Lord does not want me to have human consolations.

When I am left quiet, I resign myself to thinking about the Lord, and his will, trying to overcome opposing temptations. But if someone, thinking to do me good, approaches me to tell me something for my relief or comfort, my heart aches and my eyes fill with tears. I even feel ashamed to say that, but how can I hide it? I would like to be strong, strong as iron, and to the contrary I feel as weak as a straw. It's also a test from the Lord that these thoughts, which I would like to keep far away, always come back persistently.

---

[39] Chapter 37 of the third book of Thomas à Kempis's *The Imitation of Christ* is entitled, "Pure and Entire Resignation of Self to Obtain Freedom of Heart."

[40] the abbess: parenthetical insertion by the Italian editor.

Yesterday Reverend Father Abbot came and spoke with the doctor, who told him that it is not possible to reduce the therapy to every fifteen days, but in a month it will be possible to reduce it to every eight days, then after seven or eight months, to intervals of fifteen days. I cannot ask that you take me back now that the treatment must be done every five or six days, but, in any case, I hope that I won't be kept here for seven or eight months.

I'm also upset about the idea that the community must spend thirty-five lire per day, as I've heard. The Lord, who sees all and knows all, will consider this too so that the community doesn't have to suffer through my fault.

My dear Mother, pray much that I don't lose my religious spirit. That's my one great fear, my biggest fear, because I feel so weak and able to fall at any moment.

The Lord will help me, because he never abandons those who put all their confidence in him. I also expect the help of your prayers.

The fever stopped for two or three days but resumed last night, and this evening I still have a slight fever. I think that it must be the effect of the treatment. I realized that the distaste for food comes from fever.

These rose leaves were blessed and distributed at the Mass of Saint Rita. If you want to keep them, disinfect them, because I touched them with my hands.

Grottaferrata, June 23, 1938

My good Mrs. Sagheddu,[41]

The Lord, who so honored and privileged you in asking your daughter to make her his bride, now seems to hasten the wedding.

Dear good lady, let me explain: Sister Maria Gabriella, who has always enjoyed excellent health, began to turn pale after a cold, but

---

[41] To the mother of Gabriella: note by the Italian editor.

the doctor said it was nothing. But that change of color impressed me, and I arranged another visit. The doctor found a bit of phlegm and said that it seemed of no importance, but to be sure I wanted a radiograph. I asked the sisters to accompany her to the hospital, and the doctors examining her there were of the same opinion as our doctor. Nevertheless, the results of the radiograph showed a slight haze in the right lung.

It was decided to treat it right away with pneumothorax in a sanatorium, which the doctors claimed would lead to a complete and immediate recovery. Instead, the pneumothorax had the opposite outcome as, unfortunately, often happens, and since she begged to come back, I gave her permission. It was for me a great sorrow, because your daughter is among the best, and I love her very much because of her great virtue.

However, knowing that Sister Maria Gabriella had offered herself to the Lord for one of the noblest causes, to hasten the union among the dissident churches, I realized that the Lord has accepted the offer.

She herself told me, "since the day I offered myself I haven't felt very well." This was at the end of January, but we did not realize it until April, although I had dispensed her from the Lenten fast, finding her a bit pale, as I said.

Good Lady, I know the pain caused by my saying this: I know it from the pain that I myself feel. But with the eyes of faith, see that your daughter is ready for the upcoming heavenly and divine nuptials and weep like a mother who cries when an earthly husband asks for your daughter and takes her to his country. They are tears, but I would say tears of joy thinking about the happiness of the daughter.

Now I am certain that Sister Maria Gabriella is happy: she is quiet, serene, and deeply content. The doctor says, "It may be that she will recover." But I do not believe so; if the Lord calls, it does not matter how robust her constitution is. We forced her to eat as much as she could. But she cannot tolerate meat any more, or cheese, or bread. She still takes a lot of milk and four eggs, but all this is only for the sake of obeying—and fruit also—although she does not have any appetite.

Dear good Lady, although your daughter does not want me to tell you this, in order not to make you suffer, I wanted to warn you. But *do not grieve like those who have no faith. I dare say that your daughter is an excellent religious, now that I see the sentiments with which she suffers. I dare to say she is a holy religious: the sisters of the novitiate envy her admirable disposition.*

How many more months will this sickness last? It is God's secret.

Do not worry, because your daughter lacks nothing, and if you write to her, do it like a mother worthy of such a daughter.

With religious affection,
Sister Maria Pia

34. To her Mother

Grottaferrata, July 6, 1938
Praise to Jesus and Mary!

Dearest Mamma,

I was very happy to hear your response to the letter of Reverend Mother. I was convinced in fact that your heart would not refuse this last sacrifice. I know that an outburst would be only natural, and you would feel the need to cry, but after the first few moments you would throw everything into the heart of Jesus like a blazing furnace that consumes everything. As for my health, I will not deceive you with a false hope of recovery. Instead of making me well, the care that was given to me at the sanatorium has hastened the sickness, because when I came back from the treatments I was almost always worse. I don't want you to worry at all praying for my healing; rather, pray that the Lord does in me what is for his greater glory. I am happy to be able to suffer something for the love of Jesus. My joy becomes great when I think that the time of the true wedding approaches.

The Lord, as you know, has always favored me with special graces, but now with this disease he has done something greater than all the others. I have totally abandoned myself into the hands of the Lord, and I have gained so much.

I feel that I love my Spouse with all my heart, but I want to love him even more. I want to love for those who do not love, for those who despise him, for those who offend him. In short, my desire is nothing other than love. People in the world say we are egoists who lock ourselves up in a convent and only think of ourselves. That is false. We live a life of continual sacrifice to the point of immolation for the salvation of souls. What joy on the day when these miserable snares of the body will dissolve and I can go to contemplate face to face the Heavenly Bridegroom. My happiness is so great, and no one can take it away. And it is greater than that enjoyed by the rich in their palaces, because perhaps even as they enjoy themselves, they have death in their hearts.

There is no greater happiness than to be able to suffer something for the love of Jesus and the salvation of souls. You too be happy, Mother, and thank the Lord for this great grace that he has given to you and me.

The Lord took from your home this little flower of the field and transplanted it in the cloister, and now he wants to transport it to the gardens of heaven. Be glad and contented, Mother and family, because I am happy, and I also want you to be.

I cannot forget any of you, for that would be failing in my duty. When the news of my passing reaches you, don't respond in the nonsensical way typical of Dorgali, closing yourselves up for prolonged weeping; rather bless and thank the Lord, and the next day go to Communion and say a prayer for me. When I am up there, I'll intercede for you, and the Lord who is so good will console you in your pain and will send his heavenly blessings upon you.

Don't think that I am not being taken care of; indeed everybody gives me so much attention. Reverend Mother is so good that she doesn't spare any effort and tries in every possible way to bring relief. She comes every day to the infirmary to visit me, which is a great sacrifice for her, because we are more than fifty nuns and she must attend to all of us. No maternal heart could surpass the love and attention that she shows me.

Pray much for her: she has a right to your prayers because she sacrifices so much for me.

And now, Mamma, I ask forgiveness for all the failures and offenses that I may have caused while I was with you, and I also ask for forgiveness from all the family and from my aunt. From you, my Mother, I await your blessing. I ask you to pray for me that I may bear peacefully all the suffering that the Lord may be pleased to send me. Be resigned and rejoice in the Lord. Do not remain oppressed by pain but be happy, as I told you, and bless God for all that he does.

Remember me to the rest of the family and all our relatives. I embrace you in the Heart of Jesus.

> Your daughter
> Sister Maria Gabriella

I send you this photograph, which I don't need any more.

Grottaferrata, July 9, 1938

Good and dear Mrs. Sagheddu,

I have just received your second letter, and for three days I have had here a letter from Sister Maria Gabriella, but I did not find time until now to write a note to accompany it.

She spent a week that was somewhat better: she had a lower fever and she slept. Perhaps that is due to the prayers of her mother! But it is not the kind of improvement that we can trust in. Moreover, she is so calm and happy! One day she told me, hearing from me that her sisters in the novitiate were praying novenas, "With all these prayers and this attention they will not let me die! Actually, I am happier to go with the Lord—but as he wishes!"

Do not worry, Madam, I will keep you informed, and if it is still possible, I will ask Sister Gabriella to write to you, although it costs her much effort.

I thank the Lord that the mother is worthy of her daughter. Pray very much for her, that the holocaust will be worthy of God. Sister

Gabriella tells me that she will try to eat some cookies in order to please you. If you wish, send a pound, but not more. Here, too, we gave them to her, but she has hardly any appetite. Thank God she still takes milk, eggs, and fruit. And the Lord permits that she is offered special things like bananas and other treats, which make her think of the delicacy of Providence.

I thank you, and I will write. Sincerely yours,

 Sister Maria Pia

Nashdom Abbey
July 15, 1938

Reverend Mother Abbess,

My dear friend, the Reverend Couturier of Lyons, has granted me the privilege of reading your letter of December 1937, in which was recounted the wonderful offering and death of Mother Immacolata.

I dare to hope that you will allow me to tell you how deeply moved I have been by all that you wrote to the Reverend Priest.

I am an Anglican priest, a member of a Benedictine community established in the Church of England; among its main tasks the community works for the reunion of Anglicans with the Roman Catholic Church. So you can understand how the immense love of Mother Immacolata struck me to the depths of my heart.

The visible acceptance of her offering by the good Lord is for your separated brothers of England a valuable encouragement to persevere in their efforts, often misunderstood and ridiculed, for the return to the fold of Peter of their Anglican brothers.

As a "body" we were torn from our Mother by the State; as a "body" we ought to and we want to return to her. I asked and will ask the good Mother Immacolata to pray for us.

She who is now in Christ certainly will not disdain the cry of hearts who want to reach the fullness of the Unity that he came to bring.

May I ask you and your community for some small token of your union of prayer with our community in your work for reunion? An image or a medal that belonged to Mother Immacolata would be a real treasure for us and a sign that she embraces us with her great charity.

It will not be long before I will speak about her life and her death to the Anglican religious sisters entrusted to my care. May her example inspire many souls to imitate her offering. In fact, is it not by means of such offerings, combined with the merits of the passion of Christ, that we will see fulfilled the visible unity of all Christians in one body under one head?

Please accept my most humble religious respects.

> Your humble servant in Christ,
> Benedict Ley

35. To Father Basilio Meloni

Grottaferrata, July 15, 1938

Dear Reverend Father,

I always remember you and the good that you have done for me, so I consider it my duty to write a final word of thanks and express to you once more my gratitude. I beg you not to look too much at my handwriting, because my hand goes a bit on its own. The Lord has permitted me to contract a disease (Reverend Mother will explain), which I hope will lead me to the eternal nuptials.

Therefore I would like to show my gratitude once again. Thank you so much, Reverend Father, for caring for my spirit from its first awakening to the true life, and for leading it on the way that the Lord inspired, which has always been fruitful to my soul. Thank you for having shown such careful attention for my vocation and for having fortified it for the ordeals of life since it was first born.

Oh, my vocation! If my dream came true, I feel a great part of it is due to you who concerned yourself so much with it, even with my family. If I am in this blessed shelter, seeking the Lord, certainly I owe everything to you. My heart overflows with gratitude, but words are too poor to express what is felt in the soul. The Lord is so good that he will reward you for what you have done for my poor soul. But since you were the first to work in this arid land, you must be the first to reap the benefits. When I'm up there, if it pleases the Lord to take me, I will intercede for you, and the good Lord will not fail to bring down upon you his heavenly blessings. I am happy, and my happiness is truly great. What a joy to be able to suffer something for the love of Jesus and for souls. I made a great act of abandonment into God's hands and heart, and my soul found itself in deep peace and great joy. When I think of the blessed day when these poor ties to the body will dissolve and I can go up there to embrace the heavenly Bridegroom, then my joy and my happiness go beyond anything on earth. I hope to be your first spiritual daughter to die as a nun, and so I commend myself to your prayers to be purified and sanctified before the Bridegroom arrives. I was hoping, as you promised me, to be able to see you again on this earth, but if this is not possible, we will certainly meet again in Heaven.

Please accept my regards, and I ask your paternal blessing.

> Your daughter in Christ,
> Sister Maria Gabriella Sagheddu

[To Dom Benedict Ley]

> Grottaferrata, July 18, 1938

Very Reverend Father,

I was moved by your letter! Anything that touches the interests of Christ, of Christ adored, is done in order to move us. The union of the churches is so dear to Christ! How much he is to be loved! I hear through your lines that you belong to the small group of his friends, to those who know his intimate thoughts and desires. That his promise "et manifestabo ei me ipsum"[42] *has come true in you!*

---

[42] "I will love him and manifest myself to him"; see John 14:21.

Our dear Mother Immacolata has left a perfume of examples and memories. This year a young professed choir nun, just twenty-four years of age, asked to make the same offering. Like last year, I read in our chapter meeting the invitation[43] of your friend, Father Couturier; therefore I gave her permission and then almost completely forgot about it.[44]

Now that sister is in the infirmary, suffering from pulmonary tuberculosis, she who was one of the strongest, without anyone in her family having been subject to the same disease.

"Since the day of my offering I have not spent a day without suffering," she told me much later, when I was worried and wondering where this disease came from. Then I seemed to remember that it was she, in January, who begged me to let her offer her life for the Union.[45] And then when I asked her about it, she gave me the reply just mentioned.

Mother Gabriella—a beautiful daughter, pure, serene as an angel. During the novitiate she did not disobey once. She was gifted with an uncommon intelligence and an extraordinary memory; she used these to be "faithful!" Forgetting herself, she went about silently and unnoticed, and only now that the Lord calls do I realize what a treasure she is.

Easter Monday she was taken to the sanatorium for a simple X-ray. They kept her for forty days, lavishing on her all the necessary care, and she returned suffering as if she had been ill for two years. The treatment of pneumothorax had the opposite effect, as often happens, that is, it advanced the disease.

I do not know how many years or months the good Lord will leave her here. She wants the wedding; she wrote an admirable letter to her mother. Very simple and very calm, she seems to implement in

---

[43] for a prayer for unity

[44] Persons offering their life for Christian unity would multiply in the years following the death of Gabriella: in this respect we refer the reader to E. M. Sironi, "Preghiera e conversione all'unità. Il messaggio e la testimonianza di Paul Couturier e Maria Gabriella Sagheddu," in *Nicolaus*, Fasc. 1/2, 2000.

[45] of the churches

full a sentence of Saint Bernadette: "I no longer worry about those things that concern me."[46] Never a complaint in the midst of her sufferings; she has reached such a point of abandonment to the good pleasure of God, which demonstrates the very action of God on this soul of election.

I go to see her every night, and I confess that this is for me a joy, strength, and true spiritual relief. Pray for her and recommend her to the prayers of your sisters. Help her with her preparations for the nuptials; I am sure that she will reciprocate what you give. I hope she will glorify her Jesus and that he may glorify her for himself.

Reverend Father, may you be blessed in your good will and your desires.

August 1

Excuse me, it is only today—the feast of Saint Peter in Chains—that I resume writing this letter, begun on the day that yours arrived. So I thought a lot about you this morning and I asked the chapter to offer these days of Saint Peter, in which there is a commemoration of Saint Paul, for the separated brethren.

For you Peter is still in chains! But you already belong to the soul of the Catholic Church, and perhaps more so and better than many Catholics, even practicing Catholics.

I accept wholeheartedly the union between our two communities, also including those of your sisters, for whom I feel a great spiritual sympathy. As a sign I am sending you, as you wish, the small crucifix of our dear Mother Immacolata and two of her pious images. Allow me to add other pictures that I love very much.

Since I received your letter, every morning during Mass I invite your good guardian angels and those of your sisters to the divine banquet. Christ is our common and infinite treasure; I tell them to

---

[46] Bernadette Soubirous, 1844–1879, was favored by apparitions of the Virgin Mary at Lourdes. Her prayer to the cross is especially remembered: "You are the tree of life, the mysterious stairway that joins earth to heaven, and the altar on which I want to sacrifice myself, dying for Jesus."

take this bread of life and bring it to you. I think this is the best means of union and communion. May Jesus grant that soon you may enjoy this bread "*omne delectamentum in se habentem*,"[47] and he, in whom nothing is impossible, will respond to your desire.

Our dear Mother Immacolata is our bond of union. Her small crucifix is enriched with an indulgence granted by Pope Pius X (a unique indulgence, which only three religious have the faculty to apply). May you benefit from it someday, and later I will explain how. If you would like to send us as a sign of unity a sheet with the names of your community, you can send it by public post and in this way enable a spiritual exchange between our communities.

Thanks again for your good and lovely letter, and kindly accept my humble and religious good wishes.

> Yours humbly in Him,
> Sister Maria Pia, o.c.s.o.

36. To her Mother

> Grottaferrata, July 21, 1938
> *Viva Jesus and Mary!*

Dearest Mamma,

The other day I received your dear letter, and I was glad to receive news of you. Yesterday the cookies that you sent arrived, and I thank you very much. I tasted them and found that they taste the same as when I was in Dorgali, and they're so good. As to my health these days, I am much better. Thanks be to the Lord for everything. I am always happy to do God's will, whatever it may be, and this is my joy, my happiness, and my peace. Reverend Mother is so good and does not spare any effort or sacrifice that would give me relief or pleasure. My sisters in the novitiate only pray that they absolutely want to see me back together with them.

---

[47] "containing every delight within it"

Oh! How good it is to live in the house of the Lord, where there is one heart and one soul.

But I don't mean to say that at home I didn't always enjoy peace and quiet; on the contrary, in this regard I can testify that our family has always been a model to the neighbors. I thank you very much, Mamma, for accepting so well this sacrifice. I am happy not only to offer myself, but to be offered again by my loved ones as a host of holocaust to be consumed, if it pleases God, for the salvation of souls. I understand your pain, Mamma, and I pity you, but just think: the greater the sacrifice, the greater the reward we will receive above. Do you think that I remain impassive to your pain? Oh, no! In reading your letter, my heart was bleeding, and tears fell from my eyes as your pain became mine. I cannot understand how there are people who dare to say that when we leave our family to become nuns we forget them. Our love is rather different than at the beginning because it is supernaturalized, but, in reality, it is stronger than before. How could we forget our loved ones who have given us life, who have raised us with care and sacrifice, who have loved and still love us so much?

We have made the sacrifice of abandoning everything, but we are well compensated with happiness by living in the house of the Lord.

But if it is so beautiful to live in our monasteries, in this house of the Lord, it is even more beautiful to die here. Think, Mother, that for every religious who dies, both the choir nuns and the lay sisters must offer thirty Masses, not counting the high Mass and other prayers for the deceased.[48] Every choir nun must recite the psalter, 150 psalms that is, for the deceased, the lay sisters must say 150 *Paters or Misereres*, and in every monastery of the Order every monk or nun must say three *De Profundis*. In the monasteries of the fathers, a Mass is said every day for all the deceased of the Order, so that we are

---

[48] The so-called "Gregorian Masses" are offered in suffrage for the deceased, a practice that first appeared in writing by Pope Gregory the Great in *The Dialogues*, 4.57.14.

assured that they will pray for us in perpetuity. But it is not only we who enjoy all these privileges; so do our relatives. The entire month of November is dedicated with special prayers for our deceased relatives, friends, and benefactors of the Order. They are remembered specifically that month with an Office, Mass, and solemn Vespers, and every religious must say ten psalters for these deceased, which comes to fifteen hundred psalms. With all this, doesn't it seem beautiful and sublime to die in our Order? I've described these things at length, and now I want to tell you something that you will be happy to know. Last week Mr. and Mrs. Muceli came to visit me. I was pleased by their visit because they were so kind to me during the journey, treating me like their daughter.

They were also very happy to see me, and they even told me that I didn't appear to be sick.

The Lord is so good that he covers the effects of the disease with a veil. They told me they would write to Dorgali and would send a note to you, and I hope that they will keep their promise. This was also a consolation for me.

When I think of the tenderness and delicacy with which the Lord treats me every day in different ways, my heart melts and I am filled with a great joy.

So then I say, my God, if you treat me so delicately on this miserable earth, how will it be when I come up there to enjoy you in Paradise? My mother, my rejoicing is great, and I feel that it can't be compared to any good or joy of this world.

I am grateful to Maria Mereu, and I thank her so much for her prayers, while I myself will pray for her.

I greet everyone in the family, and I embrace you in the heart of Jesus. Send my greetings to our family and friends and especially to my Godmother Michela. Again I embrace you, and I am always your daughter.

    Sr. Maria Gabriella

Take no heed if my thoughts are not put in order, because I fish into my sack and write what comes to mind.

Grottaferrata, undated

Dear Mrs. Sagheddu,

Thank you very much for the cookies, which have pleased your daughter so much. Truly an unexpected improvement has happened. She has been almost without any fever all day: she eats and even had a little bread.

She feels much better. I do not know what to think, except to trust in the immense love that God has for us and especially for this beautiful soul, and not to demand anything except the fulfillment of his designs for his greater glory.

Sister Maria Gabriella continues to be calm, serene, happy, and always edifying; it is a pleasure to be with her, because one feels that she is always with the Lord. For now do not worry, dear lady, I will keep you informed. Thank you so much for the prayers for me—that is a real charity.

Sister M. Pia

Nashdom Abbey, August 6, 1938

Very Reverend Mother,

I do not know how to thank you for your letter, which I received yesterday, the Dedication of Mary. It is a great consolation for us to note that you accept the union of prayer between our two communities, including the sisters under our direction. The father abbot asked me to present his most respectful homage and his thanks for your kindness. He wants me to tell you of our unworthiness for such favors. We are a community still young, and there is little that we can give in return! But your solidarity will procure for us good inspirations to try to grow in the spirit of Saint Benedict, and with fidelity to our vows we hope to obtain from God the great grace of Christian unity, for which we pray and work. . . .

Last June a conference was held at Nashdom with five Jesuit priests and six Anglicans. The Jesuits did not come without the knowledge of Cardinal Hinsley, archbishop of Westminster, and in like manner, the arrival of Anglican priests was not unknown to the archbishop of Canterbury. This conference is not an official meeting of representatives of the Catholic Church, nor of the Anglican Church, but within a few years it could become so. Its purpose is to advance the cause of Unity, since the two churches suffer from their separation in the work of the conversion of England. One of our fathers, Dom Gregory Dix, wrote drafts of articles for our magazine Laudate, in which he explains the historical origins of the papacy.

I cannot tell you how much I have been moved by what you told me of Mother Maria Gabriella. I will pray for her and ask others for their prayers. It is a great joy to know anything about her. It could be that she cannot recite her Office, and in that case, I could say it in her place. In doing so, I will feel more united to her. . . .

Allow me to address a few words and a picture for Mother Maria Gabriella, as a souvenir of my prayers according to her intentions: I do so with the permission of the father abbot. I also send a list of the monks of our community and a postcard for you, signed by father abbot.

My sincere thanks for the beautiful image of Christ on the Cross, "Mecum eris in Paradiso."

I already have a foretaste of the pleasure of receiving the small crucifix of Mother Immacolata and other images of which you spoke to me that have not yet arrived.

You can be sure that we always retain this sign of our union with you and your community. A love like yours destroys the prejudices against Rome, rooted in too many Anglicans. If all Anglicans could experience your charity, the wall of separation would fall into dust.

Please accept, Reverend Mother Abbess, the expression of my most humble religious sentiments, along with confirmation of my union with you in divine charity.

>Your most humble and unworthy servant in Our Lord,
>Benedict Ley

Nashdom Abbey, August 6, 1938[49]

Your charity will allow one of the separated brethren to thank you from the bottom of his heart for the offering that you recently made for unity.

This closely resembles the passion of the Savior, in which he clearly shows the thirst he has for his Father and the thirst that he has for us. While you offer yourself incessantly to the divine Love—and may this love be fully glorified in you—you will have the joy of knowing that your separated brothers are attracted to the most sacred heart of Our Lord, because he said, "For when I am lifted up from the earth, I will draw all to myself."

From now on when reciting the Divine Office, I will do it in your name, in union with you; or rather, I will try to offer myself to Christ so that his prayer for you will be reproduced in me. May he fill you, Reverend Mother, with himself so that the divine life of the Holy Trinity, so rich and beautiful, can be manifest and glorified in you. What a wonderful thing to be called by the One who lives in us and reigns over us!

May the holy Virgin, your Mother and ours, who with Jesus and with you suffered in our place, be next to you as she stood beside the Cross.

You can count on her.

> *Your poor separated brother,*
> *Benedict Ley*

Nashdom Abbey, August 8, 1938

Reverend Mother Abbess,

I want to thank you with all my heart for the little crucifix of Mother Immacolata, for the beautiful postcards of Christ on the cross, and for the images that belonged to Mother Immacolata. They reached their destination today.

---

[49] Letter of Dom Benedict Ley to Sister Maria Gabriella.

May the Good God, whose mercy suggested to you this act of charity towards us, reward you.

Your humble and unworthy servant,
Benedict Ley

37. To her Mother

Grottaferrata, August 17, 1938

Dearest Mamma,

Many days ago I received your dear letter, and I was very glad to get news from you. God will certainly reward you for the love and resignation with which you have embraced this cross that he sent me. As for my health, thank the Lord, I am a little better, but the disease is irreversible, and we don't know what the Lord wills to do for me. Remain firm in your disposition of abandonment to the will of God, and bless him always for whatever he arranges for me. Forget that I'm sick and think only of the Lord to thank him and bless him for the graces and gifts he gave me.

I am always contented and, although sometimes I suffer, that does not prevent me from being in the joy of the Lord. I want you to know that at the end of last month Father Meloni came to visit us. He was very happy, and for me as well as for the others this visit was the cause of great consolation. Mother, you wrote to me that if you could, you would have flown to come and see me. It seems that the Lord makes this impossible; therefore sacrifice to him this desire, and your crown will be adorned with a diamond still more beautiful.

The last time I forgot to write about the sisters whom you had asked about. I see Sister Andrea when I go for a walk to the vineyard or in church: she is most contented, and she conducts herself well. Reverend Mother gave permission for Sisters Rosa and Raffaella to come and visit me so that we could talk together. They are both happy and content, and they send their greetings to their families. I also see the others often when I go out, and they're happy.

I pray and I recommend you all to the Lord. I thank all those who pray for me, and the Lord will reward you. I reciprocate the greetings to the sisters Useli and Maria Mereu. With all filial affection I bid you adieu, and I embrace you in the Heart of Jesus.

Greetings to my brother, sister, and all the relatives.

>Your daughter,
>Sister Maria Gabriella

>Grottaferrata, August 17, 1938

Good and dear Mrs. Sagheddu,

Sister Maria Gabriella is better or at least in a stuble, "not worse," condition.

A little fever, not too much coughing, a decent appetite, and her soul is always in excellent health.

In the beginning it seemed as if this abeyance of the disease weighed on her. Now, in any case, she is happy, and her will is increasingly identified with the Lord's.

Dear lady, do not cease to pray for your daughter, so that she may always continue to grow in these great and holy dispositions.

Be tranquil, for I will keep you informed.

May Jesus and Our Lady bless you and your precious family, and may your daughter be a mediator of elect graces.

>*Humbly,*
>*Sister Maria Pia*

38. To her Mother

Grottaferrata, September 22, 1938

Dearest Mamma,

At the end of last month I received your letter, and I was glad to get news from you. I was happy that you received news of me directly from Father Meloni so that you will feel more at peace about me. Now I am feeling even better, and this makes me give thanks to the Lord. For a long time it seemed that I should have already gone to Paradise; instead the Lord still keeps me in this land of exile. Of course this means that my crown is not yet complete. I find myself in the same dispositions as before, and I thank the Lord for what he has in store for me. You as well must always strive to rise up to where the Lord has placed you, because he bestowed a great honor when he chose a bride from your family—not only that, but a favored bride, because these sufferings are nothing more than a sign of divine predilection.

I thank and will always thank and bless the Lord for what he has done for me and for you, but I feel that I can never thank him enough. In fact it is a great fortune to live in a monastery where every action, even the most insignificant, even doing nothing when commanded by obedience, brings forth great merit. You who are in the world and cannot escape from the things of the world, unburden your desires, blessing the Lord, even if it seems that for a moment his hand is heavy upon you, because he does that only for your greater good. I keep you forever in my heart, and I pray for you and all the family. I thank Maria Mereu for her prayers, which I return, and I embrace you all in the Lord.

> Your daughter,
> Sister Maria Gabriella

With religious respects. Your daughter continues to be peaceful and happy. I do not know what the Lord will do; she seems quite well.

Reverend Mother Abbess,   Nashdom Abbey, November 6, 1938

My friend Father Couturier of Lyons asked me to write in order to recommend your good prayers for the coming "Octave" in the Anglican Church. Until now the Octave was organized by the papal party of the Anglican Church, that is, those who do not see any global meeting as a body, nor the return of the Anglican Church to the bosom of the Roman Catholic Church without a full agreement on dogma and especially on acceptance of the papacy, which Rome cannot change without denying herself.

This year, when Father Couturier came to England, he suggested a broadening of the "Octave" to allow those Anglicans to join who do not desire to follow its current formula. I believe that he had in mind the situation in France, where the Protestants unite with Catholics in prayer for unity.

In our opinion he has not realized that while there are Anglicans who are waiting for a change in the doctrine of the papacy, there are French Protestants who know well that unity with Rome means accepting the papacy. He has obtained a promise from two [sic] large male Anglican communities (namely The Society of St. John the Evangelist, The Cowley Fathers, and the Community of the Resurrection, Mirfield) to organize an octave of prayer parallel to that of the Octave of the papal Anglicans. This has created a difficult and delicate situation.

Concerning the prayer for unity, a subject of so great importance, there must not be two rival observances. The pro-papal party (or papists) to which Nashdom Abbey belongs is not large and does not have much influence. It seems that it will be forced to give up its organization to those who establish the Octave as a pure and simple prayer (without mentioning the papacy that exists in the Roman Church). In this way the opportunity to highlight the rights of Saint Peter toward the Anglicans will be lost or at least very limited. It is a great benefit that the prayers for unity multiply, because to pray well is to believe in God; the more numerous the Anglicans there are who do this, the more numerous will be those who seek the truth of God.

In the very first place, it is prayer that will grant us unity. Abbé Couturier was certainly right on this idea, but since unity is not possible without the Chair of Saint Peter, it is necessary that the papal party of the Anglican Church continue to give its witness.

Therefore I humbly ask your prayers that the increase of prayers for unity, so ardently desired by Father Couturier, will not hinder the work of those who feel obliged to speak to their brethren about Saint Peter. The beginning of this new Octave on this wider basis will not take place until 1940.

Frequent and fervent are my prayers for good Mother Maria Gabriella. I have also asked others to pray.

If you think it is possible, I would very much like to know the state of her health, and if she could write me a few lines, I would keep them as a word from a person crucified with Jesus.

Do not forget to pray for our community. We are so poor that we are obliged to deal with external works with great damage to our interior life. We are in God's hands; if we do his will, we are permitted to hope in his help.

Your charity makes me think constantly of your attention for us. Excuse me if I cannot express my wishes in a more concise form. Be assured that I understand very well if you cannot acknowledge receipt of my letter. Only the fact that Christ died for me *gives me the courage to ask for your indulgence, and so I hope to hear from you again.*

Receive, most Reverend Mother, my most humble and religious respects. Reassure Maria Gabriella's mother of my prayers.

Your poor separated brother,
Benedict Ley

Grottaferrata, November 11, 1938

Most Reverend Father,

I begin by apologizing for not having written more often. Meanwhile, your pictures, your letter, and the list of your community have been for us all a cause for joy, prayer, and union.

Yes, our two families have formed an alliance. Now, on All Saints' Day our community made a kind of consecration, of alliance, of fraternity with the community of heaven, as a renewed act of faith in the communion of saints.

"All you Saints of God, you are blessed. . . . Therefore we pray that you, mindful of us, would deign to intercede for us with the Lord."

I thought this intercession extended to our allied community, our sister community of England. I was delighted to see pictures of your monastery, where in the choir is a statue of the Holy Virgin, and you tell me that you recite the Office as the Benedictines do. I am truly happy about this.

It is a great strength for us to be united, because we are at the center, very privileged from childhood, but I believe that God must follow your efforts with especially loving eyes. Your letter of the day before yesterday was for me a source of much news, including the news that you are poor in terms of material things. A good sign! We are so poor that we do not know, except for three months of the year, how to pay for our bread at the end of the month. Although we were thirty-three nuns and are now fifty-two, we are not lacking anything necessary. We have appointed our cashier and treasurer in heaven, and they do wonders. When there is a payment to make, the necessary sum of money arrives: two if we have to pay two, three if we have to pay three: thus our faith can never rest.

The person who has Jesus Christ can hope less in other people. Courage, my good father, courage! How much our heavenly Father must love you, who seek to know his Son! When I saw the design of your church and monastery, I thought: they will have this and even more. He has promised to search for you as you have searched for him.

However, you have to suffer: "As the Father has loved me, so I love you." The cross is the gift of Christ, his scepter. O bona crux!

With regard to the problem that distresses you now, I understand that it is quite delicate. But there with you is the Lord who sees your suffering and your holy concern because of the danger that his glory may be compromised. Certainly he will be able to defend his glory.

Allow me to transcribe a portion of the Revelations of Saint Gertrude:

> Jesus said to Saint Mechtilde, grieving because of her feeling of inability: "Here I am. I am at your disposal. Just say to me:

'O good Jesus, supply for what I lack.' And if you were to tell me that a thousand times a day, a thousand times I would be at your disposal as a servant."

So we shall all ask the Lord to arrange this Anglican Octave "for the greater glory of God." He will succeed; is it possible that he can be incapacitated? It is true that our sins, our infidelities, paralyze his arm, but our tears move his heart.

Mother Maria Gabriella . . . advances onward. She is a remarkable creature, humble, abandoned, generous, and so wise . . . with the wisdom of the wise. The Infirmarian tells me, "When she speaks, it is simple and measured, not a word too much, and what she says could be put into writing." As for the disease, things are going better, much better, but this bacillus is not to be trusted. For the moment she has no fever, and the cough is bearable. She is always happy, happy to suffer and happy in her vocation with the good Lord. Her eyes sparkled with joy when I told her about the offering that the Holy Father Pius XI had made of his life!

Yes, this is the center: Jesus Crucified, Victim, and around him other victims, real victims, as well, unaware of their heroism and the immense value of their offerings united to that of Christ. We remain at the center, Reverend Father, near the Host. Thus the Holy Spirit helps us in our weakness and prays for us with unspeakable groans, and prays according to God for his saints.

Very Reverend Father, please give my respectful regards to your very Reverend Abbot.

I will send you some holy cards of Christ: "mecum eris in Paradiso."

Courage my good Father, good and faithful servant of him who is faithful.

> Most humbly,
> Sister Maria Pia, o.c.s.o.

I am most appreciative of your prayers: It seems to me that Jesus listens more to yours than to ours, though we are closer to him and more pampered by him. "The Lord has bent his ear towards you."

39. To her Mother

Grottaferrata, December 18, 1938
Acclaim to Jesus and Mary!

Dearest Mamma,

A long time ago I received your letter and this month a card; I was very glad to hear that you are well, and I thank the Lord. I had also written a note to send in Sister Raffaella's letter, but it was overweight and so could not be sent. I know you've been waiting for some news from me, but I hope that you are not hurt because things have turned out this way. I thought maybe the Infant Jesus wanted the task of bringing you news about me so that it would be more welcomed and arrive in time for his birth.

Thank the Lord I am much better. Since the month of August, with the drying up of the phlegm the fever has ceased, and the other pains have decreased as well.

For a long time I thought that I would have already gone to Paradise, but on the contrary it seems the Lord has decided to extend my pilgrimage. May he always be praised in everything. In early October Mr. and Mrs. Muceli came to visit me and brought me some news from you, which I appreciated because it was brought to me personally. In your letter to me, you wrote that Salvatore left because he was recalled by the military, but then you didn't tell me anything more in your note, so I don't know if he has returned. If that is so, tell him that I am always waiting for his reply, and if he has not returned, send me his address. You wrote to me that my cousin Paolo Monni was sick, but I hope that now he is cured. When you write give me news of him.

I am doing well with this illness, but we must always be prepared for death; recently we had two earth tremors within a short time of each other, which left us feeling unsafe. Don't worry about anything, but pray that when the Lord comes he will find me prepared.

I look forward to the feast of Christmas, and I hope to spend it well with the Child Jesus, because this year I am more especially united to him through the cross. I wish that the celestial Infant will bring you and the whole family joy, peace, and holy gladness. I hope that the angels will sing around you as they sang at the holy manger: glory to God in the highest, and on earth peace to people of good will.

This Infant God teaches us many lessons that we will not perhaps ever understand fully. He, the Creator of the universe, God, humbles himself to be born in a poor stable, a place for animals where he is unknown to all. See how we are quite the opposite. We're nearly ashamed to be poor, and sometimes we would almost hide this poverty because it seems to humiliate us, and we don't recognize that this is a privilege from the Lord to make us more like him. Who would dare to rebel, thinking of the humiliation and suffering of the man-God?

My wish, my dear Mother, is for you and for all that the Divine Infant would grant you the virtues of his own cradle, gentleness, humility, and love. May this be for you a feast of holy joy and gladness in accord with him.

I wish you all a holy new year full of heavenly blessings, according to your desires.

May the Lord grant you to advance more and more in holiness and in love for him in the new year. I don't want you to become rich or to be increasingly better off, but that you become more and more holy and abandoned to the will of God, and so I always pray the Lord to give you the graces necessary for your state in life. I also wish that you will always desire this for me: to become increasingly holy and grow continuously in love with the divine Bridegroom, from whom I received so many graces and predilections, and that you will pray for this.

At the cradle of the infant Jesus I'll be united with you in thought and soul, and through him, I greet and embrace you all. Greetings to our relatives, my Godmother Michela, Maria Mereu, and the homes of Sr. Rosa and Sr. Andrea. Every day—at least at Mass—I see them, and today Sr. Rosa also came to the infirmary to put in the nails for the Stations of the Cross.

Once again I write farewell to you all and ask you to bless me.

> Always your daughter,
> Sister Maria Gabriella

Pray always for Reverend Mother. The picture of the Resurrection is for Maria Mereu.

40. To Father Basilio Meloni

Grottaferrata, December 19, 1938

Reverend Father,

Reverend Mother told me to write this note in order to give you some news about myself. I thought I would be already in heaven, and instead it seems that the Lord is prolonging my pilgrimage on earth.

May his divine will be done always and in everything. I have never regretted living in abandonment, and I am certain that's how it will be for the future. I am sure that Jesus will do what is best for his greater glory and my sanctification. Now I'm a lot better than when you came to see me. Since August I haven't had a fever, and there have been other improvements, although there is no lack of small daily problems.

But why be in the infirmary if you're not suffering anything?

Without combat we won't gain a victory, and without suffering we can't expect a crown. Jesus has chosen me as privileged in his love by giving me suffering to make me more like him. I am happy for this, and I thank him. I feel that I'll never quite understand the love that Jesus shows me in offering me this cross. Of course according to our nature the disease is a little humiliating, and nature puts up a fight for a few moments, but love and grace soon overcome the natural humiliations, which become the dearest delights of the soul.

Thank you, Reverend Father, for the visit that you granted me, and which did me good. I ask pardon for not having even said goodbye before your departure because I didn't know anything about it. Actually the next day I was expecting you for Mass, but Reverend Mother told me that you had left right away. Thank you for having sent news to my mother; certainly, from what she wrote, you did her a lot of good. I recommend myself very much to your prayers so that I can follow the path opened up for me by the Lord, and I will do the same for you.

Please bless me and accept my respectful regards.

Your daughter in Christ,
Sister Maria Gabriella

41. To Father Basilio Meloni

Grottaferrata, February 1, 1939
Viva Jesus and Mary!

Reverend Father,

Reverend Mother read to me a part of the letter you wrote to her, and I was very impressed.

I sensed from your words that the Lord tries you and that you have much to suffer. We offered our consecration, and the Lord did us the honor to take us at our word. I am sure that our sufferings will be for the greater glory of God, more profitable for us and for the salvation of souls.

Father, let us lift our spirits and our souls to the Lord, for he will comfort us and will not abandon us in tribulation. All things work together for good for those who love the Lord, says the apostle. Forgive me, Father, if I talk this way, but your words have revealed to me a little dejection and mistrust, and so the Lord inspired me to write in this way, and I have obeyed the inspiration. I always pray for you, and I hold you in my heart, and I offered my Communion today for this intention. I also pray for the two aspirants to our way of life, and I hope that the Lord, if it is to his glory, will do everything.

I ask pardon for my boldness and ask for your blessing. Please accept my filial respects,

    Sister Maria Gabriella

42. To Father Basilio Meloni [50]

    Grottaferrata, February 2, 1939

Reverend Father,

Yesterday I wrote you a note that at present distresses me. I'm sure that I interpreted your words poorly, and therefore I spoke shamefully and with little respect. Since Reverend Mother had to send another letter, I believed it was my duty to write you again to ask your pardon. I didn't understand well the words that certainly struck me most in your letter, in which, with infinite anguish, you asked for the help of prayers. But I'm sure that with these words you wanted to express the endless anguish that pours into our hearts from the heart of Christ when we see him offended and mistreated, and when we see souls lost while we do all we can to save them: they jump head first into the abyss forever. The Lord made me understand very well that as you already are quite used to such trials you wouldn't let these conquer you.

I beg your pardon. Excuse me for having spoken to you so badly and without respect: as you can see I am still the same. I have a weak head, and I speak without considering what I'm saying. Of course, I hope you will forgive this reckless talk and pray for my conversion. I will also continue to pray for you.

Please accept my respects and best wishes in the heart of Jesus, as I ask you to bless me,

    Your daughter in Christ,
    Sr. Maria Gabriella

---

[50] Mother Pia reprimanded Gabriella for what she wrote to Father Meloni in the previous letter, offering him her "advice"; therefore this is a letter of apology.

43. To her Mother

Grottaferrata, March 25, 1939

Dearest Mamma,

Although in our Order we do not write letters during Lent, Reverend Mother wanted me to send this note to you just to give you a little news. It has pleased the Lord for me to remain almost always in the same state as when you wrote the other time. I am still in the infirmary because my strength does not allow me to work with the others, and this disease demands some separation from others. I lack nothing of what might be needed for a sick person, and even the superiors compete to bring me some relief, so therefore I can tell you that they all treat me like a queen and not as the miserable person that I am. Do not feel sorry or sad for me, because I'm always glad and contented with all that the Lord arranges.

I got your Christmas card and your letter, for which I am very thankful. When you write postcards don't write more than five words, because otherwise they will be taxed. Since it is my duty and my job to pray for others more than anything else, I always pray for you and commend you to the Lord so that he might help you in all your needs and make you grow increasingly in holiness. I wish a good and holy Easter to you, the family, and the relatives; may it be happy, full of grace and heavenly blessings. Rise with Jesus to new life and rush with him more forcefully in the ways of love and abandonment. Pray for me so that Jesus may find me more and more worthy of Him.

Sincere regards and an embrace to all, in the Lord.

Your daughter
Sister Maria Gabriella,

Grottaferrata, March 29, 1939

Dear Mrs. Sagheddu,

With longing of the soul, and with the progressive advancement of the disease, your daughter begins her way to Paradise. Calm, serene, always happy, always ready to sacrifice; really she seems more like an angel than a creature of this world. Do not think I exaggerate, or say this because you are her mother. It is truly so, even more so than I can express.

Certainly it is a blessing for you and for the family, and it will be even more so when the Lord of heaven and earth arrives to bring her to reign with Him.

Dear and good lady, pray for your daughter, so that her virtue—dare I say her holiness, a holiness made of joy, humility, and surrender to God—may continue to grow more and more.

Humbly,
Sister Maria Pia, O.C.R.

Holy Saturday, April 8, 1939

Good and dear Mrs. Sagheddu,

Your daughter said to me a few days ago: "It came into my mind that perhaps he will take me as a Paschal lamb."[51] Perhaps it will be so. She declines rapidly; already last Friday we gave her Extreme Unction, and today Holy Viaticum. She wanted this so much! She was so happy and she is still happy. When she says, "How good the Lord is," and smiles and looks up with her usual gesture, she is transformed and she seems to me like an angel.

Dear lady, I would like to please you with her photograph! But we are cloistered; no one can come in, and even those (here) who knew a bit of photography would not be able to do it. Make this sacrifice too! She looks just like Sister Therese of the Child Jesus, with those big eyes that makes us think of Paradise. She is calm, serene, and

---

[51] Gabriella died on the fourth Sunday of Easter.

happy! She takes some cookies with mineral water, and we put an orange in the water as a drink; she can take them and smiles because they are from her home.

Madam, I am sure that the Lord, for the sake of your daughter, will bless you, your family and many others!

It could be further prolonged, I do not know; the Lord knows and does all things so well! Let him do it, and let us give thanks.

>   With affection,
>   Sister Maria Pia, o.c.r.

Friday at 5:00 a.m. (April 21, 1939)
My dear Mrs. Sagheddu,

I write here, near your daughter, who is calm and often smiling, always sweet, and almost motionless before the "honeymoon." Last night I was here as well, for it is the end of her pilgrimage, and although this kind of disease can be prolonged beyond all expectations, it can also bring surprises.

Around eleven o'clock it seemed to me, judging from her breath, that the Lord would take her, so we called the Reverend Father Chaplain, a truly holy priest, who is full of zeal and love despite his seventy years. When she saw him, Sister Maria Gabriella welcomed him with a smile full of holy joy. She received Communion at midnight and then recovered. We are here around her, praying.

Just now I said to her, "I am writing to your Mamma." "Thank you," she replied. She joins herself to the prayers with her mind and, though suffering, when asked if she agrees to suffer more if God wills it, she immediately says yes. When the Lord admits her to eternal union, I will send you a telegram. Rejoice then, rejoice and be more thankful than ever: you will have your daughter closer to you than when she was with you and more than she is now.

May the Lord bless you. Thank you for your letter to Sister Gabriella and to me.

44. Two pictures of Sister Gabriella Sagheddu

Pictures representing the Holy Face of Jesus Crucified with the indication of the author: Brother Marie Bernard, the sculptor, and the place, Abbaye Grande Trappe–Orne.

Words written by Maria Gabriella: "I am with you."

> Your daughter,
> Sister Maria Gabriella

Holy Saturday, April 7, 1939

2. For Giovanna

I pray the Lord to bless you and your family, and with the Lord I am united with you.

> Your sister,
> Sister Maria Gabriella

Easter, 1939

45. To her Mother[52]

Dearest Mamma,

I write these lines to send you my last thoughts and my last farewell. The Divine Bridegroom has renewed the invitation, and the longed-for day approaches. I do not say the day of my death, but the day when, loosed from the bands of this miserable flesh, I can finally move on from this life to the happy and blessed life of heaven. The separation from the body is not a death but a transition to real life.

---

[52] "To be delivered after death." The note was written in pencil by Mother Pia on the top edge of the signed letter, drafted by the dying nun with very firm handwriting.

Rejoice, oh my Mother, because there will be no more enclosure, and I, although you will not see me, I will come and visit you and hug you so much, as my love for you grows more and more. Be at peace because up there I will be much more useful to you than I could be here; there I will see clearly all your needs, and I will intercede more with the Lord. Do not cry and do not make a fuss as they do in Dorgali, because I would be greatly displeased.

I wish indeed that the same day you receive the news, you will all go to Mass and Communion and pray for me and thank the Lord very much for the graces he has given me and for his predilections in my regard.

I hope that Salvatore and my brother-in-law have fulfilled their Easter duty, but, if not, I recommend that they do so as soon as possible, at least as my last wish. I pray so much for them.[53]

I still recommend that you remain tranquil and happy in the Lord. Pray for me and commend me to the prayers of our relatives and acquaintances to whom I am sending with you my final greeting. One last time I ask everyone for forgiveness for any offenses that I may have caused. I embrace you tightly in the heart of Jesus, together with all the family.

> Always your daughter,
> Sister Maria Gabriella

Wednesday, April 26, 1939

Dear Mrs. Sagheddu,

How much you must have waited for this letter from me! With it comes the last letter written by your daughter, who wrote it according to my advice, and she agreed that I would send it to you after her passage to the heavenly kingdom.

---

[53] This is the brother-in-law who attended the ceremony of the beatification of Gabriella on January 25, 1983, and received Communion from the hands of the Supreme Pontiff.

From Thursday the twentieth, Mother Maria Gabriella had a significant worsening. Already since Easter we were keeping vigil with her at night, even though she did not want to disturb us. On Thursday Holy Communion was brought to her at midnight, as well as on Friday, fearing that a moment later would be too late. Saturday morning she improved before her final passage, and then she began to suffer intensely. Her body of twenty-five years and two months fought with strong resistance. But she was suffering with such docility and resignation. Consenting to acts of acceptance, love, and offering that we suggested to her, Saturday night seemed to be her last, but she was fully conscious. She asked with that small voice that was soon clear, "Communion, if possible, if possible." It was brought to her again as Viaticum. She recovered a bit. . . . But we remained all night, the nurse, two sisters, and I . . . and the Father Chaplain, who wanted to stay, despite his advanced age, not wishing to leave her without accompanying her to the last breath.

The afternoon of that Saturday was a providential occasion because we had the visit of Reverend Father Abbot, our superior, accompanied by the procurator general of the Order. The bishop also came, and he offered to give a blessing to our young patient. With pleasure he blessed her and recommended himself much to her prayers.

All during the night she suffered greatly, indeed, like a lamb.

At about 2:00 a.m., as we were reciting the Office of Matins, she calmed down completely, resumed her breath, and had the delightful expression of a child. She stayed like that for several hours, and then the suffering returned, acutely. The chaplain came after preaching to the community and asked if she wanted to receive Jesus. She calmed down, and smiled throughout the preparation, and giving thanks I repeated to her, "How good the Lord is! How the Lord loves you! Let us offer to him the dispositions of Our Lady for this last Communion." As usual she said, "How good the Lord is," and she said it now with an angelic expression that was moving.

She continued to get worse—but nearly motionless, suffering immensely, and always sweet, modest, and dignified—it continued this way until the afternoon. She looked at her hands, already pur-

plish, and smiled as much as she could, kissing the crucifix with prolonged kisses, when it was handed it to her.

At four o'clock everyone went to Vespers, and only the Infirmarian stayed on. Then she went into her agony. The sister, an excellent religious (from Bitti) pleaded with the Lord, with such great faith (she told me afterward) to extend it—until they finished Vespers and came back. After Vespers, I went to the infirmary with the whole community. The Father Chaplain came. We have the custom of ringing the bells in a certain way when someone enters her final agony. But the sisters were mistaken, and I heard the two bells ringing in celebration. In fact, it was the nuptial feast.

At half past five, very tranquilly, she ceased to breathe. She lowered her eyelids—as when she was unable to speak, to say, "Yes." Then she raised her eyelids again. She was already with her Lord, whom she loved so much that she offered the sacrifice of her young life for the union of the separated churches.

It was Good Shepherd Sunday, and the gospel spoke thus: "I have other sheep, which are not of this fold; I must bring them also." Signora, cry pure tears: you are her Mother. But give thanks, give thanks to the Lord. Yesterday we had the burial ceremony. During the night her sisters from Dorgali kept vigil in the church with the other sisters, two at a time. Now she rests in the tomb of the monastery, which is located under the presbytery, and her coffin is placed just below the altar.

Dear lady, your desire for a photograph is so right and understandable, and it has remained impressed on my mind. One day Father Chaplain tried to take one, but he managed very poorly! Nevertheless, providentially, I was able to take one when she was laid out in the choir. I could not do more—now in spirit she will be close.

I will send you a rosary that when she was sick, I put into her hands, saying that I would later send it to her mother. "Thank you," she replied gratefully. It was blessed by the late pope.

May Jesus bless you, dear Mrs. Sagheddu.

Sister Maria Pia, o.c.r.

Nashdom Abbey, April 29, 1939

Reverend Mother Abbess,

I intended to write to you immediately after receiving your card, but it was impossible.

I was sorry to learn from our Reverend Abbot of the death of Mother Maria Gabriella. Ever since I received the news that she was dying, I always prayed.

I am happy for her that God has accepted her sacrifice. I believe this is a sign of the greatness of the cause, for which he, our Jesus, the Good Shepherd, died. And he has called her precisely on the feast of the Good Shepherd, is it not so? "I have other sheep, which are not of this fold; I must bring them also, and they will hear my voice; and they will become one flock with one shepherd."

I cannot tell you how much I would appreciate some small memory of her that you could send.

I would also like to note that she went to the Lord on the Feast of Saint George, patron saint of England. It means that she will pray especially for our community and its work for the return of England to true unity.

I ask forgiveness for my delay in responding to your last letter, so full of encouragement and of faith and hope in God.

I believe that our Reverend Abbot has written to you on the subject of our concern: we fear that there may be a confused orthodoxy in our Church of England when the great synod of our bishops will discuss the great truths of the Nicene Creed.

We ask your prayers for those Anglican priests who profess loyalty to the Catholic faith to be strong so that they will not disappoint our hopes for the meeting.

I told my friend Abbé Couturier of the death of Mother Maria Gabriella. You can easily imagine how we, like you, feel united with the Holy Father Pius XII when he prays, "Da nobis pacem."

It is a true consolation to know that nothing in the world can upset all the hopes of Christians in his great prayer.

       Your humble servant in the Lord,
       Benedict Ley

Grottaferrata, May 3, 1939

Reverend Father,

After the death of our little Mother Gabriella, I feel united to your community, as never before. The night before her death, in which she suffered terribly, I put a little statue of the Virgin Mary on her bed, the same one that I have on our worktable, and at the foot of the statue your image of the Sacred Heart. I made her kiss it while she renewed her offering, and, taking her hand, I traced her signature, thinking to send it to you after her death as a remembrance. You have been so good to her, praying the night office for yourselves and for her since she fell sick.

Yes, Jesus has called her to himself on this Sunday in which we have the gospel of "Union." That fact struck us. She entered into agony at the hour of Vespers. Instead of ringing the bell at four intervals, as is our custom, they made a mistake and the two bells rang out! I noticed it, but because of the distance I was not able to remedy the situation. Perhaps the Good Lord permitted it this way: it was in fact a nuptial feast.

The little Mother has left such a record of virtue that I am asked to write a few notes for the novitiate. I do not know; I will wait for the circumstances when the Good Lord will inspire me.

Thank you for the prayers that you offered for her. Thank you. I am sure she will help you. I enclose a photograph that I tried to make as requested by her desolate mother. My good Father, pray for us so that together with your community, a bond of union will be formed after the death of Mother Gabriella.

Humbly,
Sister Maria Pia, o.c.r.

May 9, 1939

Reverend Mother Abbess,

I cannot tell you how much I was moved by your letter in which you described the death of your dear Maria Gabriella. You were very kind to return to me my religious image with her name written in her own hand, and so I thank you with all my heart.

I will always cherish the memory of this act of charity and the image that her lips have kissed before renewing her offering. It will be a help for me, I am certain! The photograph of Mother Maria Gabriella after the consummation of her sacrifice, a gift that I would never have dared to hope for, will teach me, like the crucifix, to face any sacrifice the Lord asks of me. So it will attract me to join with her in that ineffable unity that is the final end of our Christian vocation, the unity of the Blessed Trinity.[54]

If I were less imperfect, I would feel moved to make the offering that you have permitted. Meanwhile I offer what I can for the "reunion." Since 1938, I have a heart condition and consequently cannot follow the monastic life as strictly as everyone else, and occasionally I suffer from exhaustion. It is not a great thing; it is a small offering. Pray that I offer it well.[55]

---

[54] See John 17:21 22.

[55] The death of Gabriella inevitably aroused among people engaged in the ecumenical journey a desire to emulate and to ask questions about possible forms of offering for the cause. Mother Augusta Tescari writes: "Those who join Vitorchiano after having read a biography of Sr. Maria Gabriella often do so attracted to a monastic life in which the ecumenical ideal has a great part. But even those who have become acquainted with Cistercian monasticism in other ways cannot but feel the atmosphere of great interest and love for the ecumenical cause, inseparable from a genuine love for Christ and for the church, which is lived in the community. Liturgical and personal prayer for unity, supported by a fair understanding of the issue, is part of the life experience of each of us. On some special occasions, the evangelical and permanent values of monastic life that can and must make a monastery a privileged place of ecumenical and inter-religious meeting allow us to take some small and very modest initiative. I would not say, however, that this is the core of what we have inherited from Sr. Maria Gabriella. The inspiration to offer her life in sacrifice came to her personally, and in this we cannot presume to imitate her. Her offering reaches us in another way, however. Immersed in the mystery of the church, in which we contemplatives feel a bit to be the heart, it is at home, and it is among ourselves that Sr. Maria Gabriella calls us to foster unity. We are convinced that this is a real, albeit implicit, form of ecumenism." (From the report, "Il carisma di Sr. Maria Gabriella come prassi di vita comunitaria," *Convegno in occasione del 60° anniversario della morte della Beata Maria Gabriella Sagheddu*, Cagliari, Pontifical Theological University of Sardinia, April 23, 1999.)

It is great joy for me to know that you feel more united to our community. The Savior has inspired this goodness of yours to us, and he will reward you. I am quite sure that the union of prayer between Roman Catholics and Anglicans will come about one day (perhaps soon, because world events push Christians more than ever toward reunion), for the re-establishment of visible unification that today is torn apart.

I enclose a few lines for the mother of Maria Gabriella. You will know, Reverend Mother, if it will be good for her to receive it, because I do not want to be a stranger who tries to break into her pain. I hope I can be a comfort to her mother's pain, which I find so intense in your letter (my mother died in 1913, when I was only seventeen years old), but it is not possible for me not to tell her that the offering made by her daughter inspired me to greater fidelity to our Lord.

I do hope that with God's help you decide to write some memories of Maria Gabriella . . . Deo adjuvant.

I dare ask again for your prayers for a conference to be held here with the Jesuit Fathers in early June.

Our very Reverend Abbot thanks you for your letter and the photograph of Mother Maria Gabriella taken before burial, and he asked me to relate his most respectful sentiments.

Please accept, Reverend Mother, the assurance of my gratitude and the expression of my religious respect.

I remain united in prayer.

    Humbly yours in Christ,
    Benedict Ley

Dom Benedict Ley's Letter to Mrs. Sagheddu

I am an Anglican priest, a monk of an English Benedictine community. Ever since I learned of the offering of your daughter for the return of the separated brethren I have prayed for you. I hope you will allow me to tell you that the sacrifice of your daughter inspires me to greater fidelity to Christ and more intimate prayer for the reunion of all Christians under the Pope. . . . Maybe it will console you to know that the offering of your daughter has done good among Anglicans, many of whom long for a corporate reunion with Rome.

I will pray for you very much, Signora. I entrust you to the Mother of Sorrows, she who stood at the foot of the cross of Jesus and will support you and comfort you in your loss.

Excerpts of letters from Dom Benedict to Mother Pia

Nashdom Abbey, May 24, 1939

Our community has not yet received the same favors as yours, but I can affirm that I feel very much helped interiorly by the intervention of Mother Gabriella with God.

It seems to me that God will grant these favors as signs that the sacrifice she offered him is very pleasing to him.

May she continue to help us greatly by her prayers.

December 8, 1939[56]

Every week when I pray (say Mass, as I believe) for M. L'Abbé Couturier, I pray too for you and the Mother of my dear helper in Heaven, Mother Maria Gabriella.[57] *In addition I try once a fortnight to say Mass for your community—so you see I am true to our union in prayer. I am very sure that the dear little Sister Maria Gabriella aids me in secret. I pray to her and with her.*

January 10, 1940

One day I think I felt for a moment a faint smell of flowers. I was in the choir at Matins. This caused me much intimate joy. Perhaps my dear little sister in heaven was close to me then.

---

[56] Extract from Dom Benedict's original letter. For the others quoted here, we have only the earliest Italian translations.

[57] Dom Benedict refers to Father Couturier using the French title for a diocesan priest, *abbé*.

I pray the good Lord to reveal to all people his work in her soul, for his glory and for the sake of the reunion.

. . . The Lord seems to show me more and more the glory of the cross and, that in order to really live, one must die there on it with him. His grace I attribute to my little sister . . .

Because of the war, correspondence between Grottaferrata and Nashdom Abbey was interrupted from the end of March 1940 until February 1946.

Autograph Notebooks of Mother Pia Gullini

1953

Responses to Gaston Zananiri's questions[1]

☩ JM
August 13–18, 1953

Dear Sir:

Finally I have finished. Be so kind as to excuse my delay. I have before me your good and very kind letters, and I'll try to answer them. The books that Maria Gabriella possessed include one on Saint Mary Magdalen of Pazzi; that is a biography that was rather complete and was part of the novitiate library. There was also a book by Saint Alphonsus Liguori, *The True Bride of Jesus Christ*, which is always read by beginners because of its strength, clarity, and emphasis on doctrine, illustrated by many examples. It consists of two volumes, neither of which is large.

The passage of Ruysbroeck that had made an impression on her I found as a quotation in a book in the infirmary—which, I do not know. These books, after being used by the

---

[1] Or "Autograph Quinternions," to quote literally from the Italian. In response to questions asked by Gaston Zananiri, who was writing the first French biography of Sr. Maria Gabriella, M. Pia made notes on these quinternions—booklets made up of five pages folded in half. These are today in the Vitorchiano Archives.

young tuberculosis patient, were burned or relegated to a box in the attic of the infirmary.

If the author of the two biographies did not speak of them at length, it means either that they were not worth mentioning or that the books had already been destroyed. You must keep in mind that the biography was written, or at least begun, four or five months after the death of Sister Maria Gabriella and written on the spot by a novice already well known as a writer, and especially as a hagiographer, who came from a Benedictine monastery and had already practiced the Benedictine Rule, which is also that of Cîteaux. Each chapter was submitted to me, and I can assure you that I looked at it carefully for the sake of moral "truth." Several small details are not in the documents because the novice would come to me, question me on this or that point, and have the friends from Sr. Gabriella's village recount—before me—this or that particular thing that they had retained in their memory. Then, in the spirit of a person practicing her profession, she picked up the various nuances so that she could draw a true-to-life portrait with the tangible assistance of God. For that young girl, Sr. Maria Gabriella, passed by smiling, but talking very little, so that, without the "fragrances" and the "writer sent by God," she would have been forgotten, or else everything would have been said about her in ten pages.

This is to say that the two biographies have caught everything "live" whether it was from the general ambience or from the witnesses themselves.

Now after thirteen years, we can mention some passages from letters that for the sake of prudence were omitted at that time. But as a portrait of Sister Maria Gabriella, one can only reproduce that from the two biographies.

I just finished re-reading them—for you—or rather I read them for the first time, because after reviewing and correcting the original (both of them) with conscientious severity, I didn't want to read the two printed books. I didn't review the drafts, and I realize now that several inaccuracies were introduced.

Reading them between yesterday and today I find my little daughter as she was, alive, really herself, and I took note of the passages that give us a photographic image of her true character in order to copy them for you and in order to respond to your questions of today with what I said then.

May God help you as he helped Miss Maria Giovanna Dore, who had entered the Trappist monastery with the intention of not writing any more and then, by obedience, wrote on a theme—the union of Christians—that she knew much better than I, having several times heard Cardinal Lavitrano, archbishop of Palermo, the great apostle of Unity, who died six or seven years ago.[2] She wrote a book that has had six editions, not counting the two Paoline editions.

Her other books have reached only the second and third editions.

Some knowledgeable people have told me that the short biography (the Paoline edition) was a better portrait of Sister Maria Gabriella, because the author had deepened her personal knowledge of her.

Daily Timetable. The timetable that you are asking about has not changed. I will write separately about the schedule and also about her nutrition.

Work. The nature of the work is as follows. The young, according to their strength, work in vegetable gardens, where the toughest jobs are done by one or two workers, helped at that time by a donkey and now by a mule. Especially in spring there is transplanting and weeding, in summer, fruit picking, and in autumn, the harvest. When Sr. Maria Gabriella speaks of digging it was small plots of land where they continually "alternate" a legume and salad patch. Although the "hard" work would not last more than an hour or two, with small stops to rest, this is not to say that for those young people who were not used to it, it wasn't fatiguing. The other work of the

---

[2] 2 August 1950

time was sewing and other needs of the large family that constituted the community: cleaning, laundry, etc. In winter the "proficient" dedicated themselves to embroidery or painting. Sr. Maria Gabriella found it remarkably easy to succeed in everything. In the infirmary, under the guidance of Mother Michela, she made two heads of the Madonna, or rather two medallions (about fifteen centimeters in diameter) with the head of the Madonna, which could not be distinguished from those made by Mother Michela.

Numbers (in the community): Then there were around fifty, perhaps fifty-three or fifty-four, of which at any given time there were sixteen in the novitiate, but some of them left, and their place was taken by others who were entering.

Nationality: All Italian, with the exception of an elderly French nun, who died fifteen days before Sr. M. Gabriella. Between six and eight in the novitiate were from Sardinia.

Her appearance: She was beautiful, but her modesty hid her like a veil, even before entering. In the monastery, with eyes so often lowered and her head slightly leaning forward, she didn't attract attention to herself at all.

Her stature was slightly above average. She arrived when she was twenty-one years and six months of age; she died at twenty-five years and one month. Broad forehead and beautiful, bright large eyes with a deep expression and so transparent that when she came to see me, I had the impression of seeing her soul. She said hardly anything, but her total gift, her docility, absolute and deliberate, her calm personal equilibrium, humble gratitude, and affection, pure and filial: all this you could read in her eyes. And it could be read so well that I myself could not find anything to say, or very little.

Personal recollection: In this regard I remember that while I was making the annual retreat at the end of October 1938, a time when the superior does not speak to the community, I saw her go into the choir for the visit to the Blessed Sacrament, while the community was at work. I remembered that day, October 31, the eve of All Saints' Day, and in 1937 it was the feast of Christ the King, so it was the anniversary of her profession. There was a custom for the young nuns who wanted to, to go to Reverend Mother on the anniversary of their profession and renew their vows.[3] The little one (Sr. Gabriella) had been in the infirmary for five months. Reverend Mother called her and went out, motioning her to follow her. Sister Maria Gabriella was glad. She repeated the formula of the vows with her hands in the hands of the abbess; she received the ritual embrace with the answer, "God reward thee with everlasting life." She didn't say a word, but her beautiful bright eyes and her wonderfully charming smile expressed her joy and gratitude. Mother looked for a holy card and gave it to her, without herself saying a word, either, and watched her walk away, so simple, humble, and yet dignified. She [the abbess] was astonished and edified by this silence, which caused her to admire once again the deep Cistercian spirit that revealed itself more with actions than with words.

Her mouth was rather large, but her smile had a sweetness, a stunning beauty that revealed her teeth, white and straight, which manifested youth and health. The chin was broad and very strong-willed. Hers was a classic profile, and sometimes my eyes, a bit artistic, left me in admiration. I seemed to see again the plaster sculpture model that I had to copy during my student years, when I was young.

The portrait: I will give you here an explanation concerning the portrait of her profile, from which you will discern a sign of Providence.

A few months before her death, an illustrated booklet of one of the monasteries of our Order arrived.

I passed this on to Mother Tecla, the mistress of novices, who found the head of a monk—with his hood up—whose profile was exactly the same as that of Sr. Maria Gabriella. She showed this illustration to the novices, who confirmed the

---

[3] In this narrative and occasionally below M. Pia refers to herself in the third person, as *Reverend Mother*.

accuracy of her observation. Then taking that picture she went to visit little Sister Maria Gabriella as she used to do every day (since the young professed sisters remain for two or three years in the novitiate), announcing, "Sister Maria Gabriella, here is your portrait." She looked at it for a moment, shook her head, smiling, submissive, and silent. The Mistress showed it to me, but I didn't give it much attention. Then, before her death when the family begged to have a photograph of her, I was embarrassed. The good Father Chaplain (nearly seventy years old), who had recently arrived, offered to satisfy that desire. It was ten or twelve days before the death of Sr. M. Gabriella.

So we made her sit on an armchair, and doing his best with a machine that he was not familiar with, he snapped, five or six poses I believe. It was a complete failure: there was only one in which the eyes of the dying person were quite well photographed, while the nose and mouth, blurred, were impossible. Nobody could send it to the family, but it was given to a friend of the monastery, the wife of the famous painter and sculptor Biagini. She made a large oil painting, larger than life, but only the eyes were similar. First a large reproduction was made and later a smaller one. But the sisters, her companions in the novitiate (including some from her own village) absolutely refused to recognize it, and the same thing happened in her village from her family and friends.

When in 1940 the biography was published, they immediately asked for a photo. The good Mother Tecla (the Novice Mistress) repeated to me many times that I had to take advantage of the offer that Providence had sent us in advance with the portrait from the brochure. But I felt a strong aversion, and I was almost invincible about that way of proceeding, which didn't seem like the truth. Furthermore, my embarrassment increased because of their continuous insistence. One night— I was alone and praying—I took the much-discussed portrait of the young monk with downcast eyes under his hood. I cut the tip of the hood with a scissors and with a pencil I drew the forehead: Sister Gabriella was there, full of life and natural. I was very moved—and I gave in. I surrendered to God.

I sent for Ms. Biagini; I explained it to her and asked her to complete the portrait with veil and wimple. Then I went to the parlor myself (to pose as a model). The lady (Ms. Biagini) did it with talent and kindness: that is the reason that you see in this picture the face that is a photograph and the rest that is painted in watercolor, a modern genre. We reproduced the portrait. In the village, the mother and family members recognized it and were happy. The companions of her novitiate breathed a sigh of relief: "Now that is Gabriella!" But I was still saddened by something that didn't seem to me to be perfectly right.

But God himself, who is Truth, in his generosity, had provided.

Defects: It was she (or her friend) who told me the defects of her youth. In the monastery I have never heard a complaint about her or even a well-deserved reproach.

After her death, when I asked for testimonies, I remember having read of two infractions of the Rule being stressed—only two. First, she made a sign to her former sub-mistress in the novitiate as they brought out the winter blankets to the sun, and shaking them, she indicated hers, which she had woven herself. It was a kind of hand weaving typical of Sardinia. It was a useless communication according to our strict rules of silence. I think she thought it was a good way to form a relationship as the inferior with her former sub-mistress.

The second: waiting her turn near the confessional a month before her death. One of her companions, from her village, passed by: she was the one who had entered the monastery first and made the monastery known to the others. Sr. Maria Gabriella made the sign for *thank you* in a grateful and touching way. The other knew very well that she was thanking her for having opened to her, from the human perspective, the way to the monastery. Here we have another small material infraction of silence, but made necessary by gratitude! I say this to let you know her great fidelity.

Two more exceptions: Once only I reproached her severely because, despite my encouraging words, she continued to insist that she had performed her function as *invitatrix* poorly; later my words had an indelible impression of grace in her, practical and effective.

While she was in the hospital, by means of my letters, I used to complain to her maternally but strongly so that she would overcome her repugnance (the true and right supernatural motive of which I was unaware). That is all the negative elements that have been noted about her. The rest is a unanimous praise for her fidelity, which was the fidelity of love.

The splendor of these souls (Mother Gabriella and Mother Michela), which seemed quite natural while they were alive—I'm quoting the thought of Mother Tecla, which is also my thought—that splendor was appreciated in all its value only afterwards, by measuring the difference with their novitiate companions, who were also good, and then making the comparison that necessarily resulted.

Her consistency: Sister Maria Gabriella was coherent with herself. Her intelligence, her integrity, and especially her balance brought her to this naturally. On this point, her love drove her to virtue. With her even pace, dignity, and continuity, she was moving upward without ever voluntarily looking back, especially in the great trial of the hospital.

Love made her understand the necessity of this path of always going forward; it was that which constituted an aid to her strong will and her just and righteous reason, and gave her that quality of simplicity that one admired without even knowing why. *Bene omnia fecit*.[4] But, since one should always act in this way, all of this was natural. She was the first to consider it natural. God wanted to allow her to catch the attention of others, with her "fragrances."

About some quotations: Pages 149–52 of the Morcelliana edition:[5]

---

[4] "He did all things well," Mark 7:37

[5] Maria Giovanna Dore, *Dalla Trappa per l'Unità della Chiesa: Suor Maria Gabriella (1914–1939)*, foreword by Igino Giordani (Brescia: Morcelliana, 1940).

On page 149 of the Morcelliana edition there are quotations of dialogues; the second line is called "scrawls in pencil." This is what it is: about twenty days before her death I allowed her novitiate companions to meet her and greet her individually, one after the other. I was in the room, on the sidelines, in front of a table with a magazine under my eyes, listening without letting it be known. Soon I was struck by the wisdom of the words pronounced slowly and with effort by Sr. Maria Gabriella. I wanted to preserve them, but I had only one magazine and a pencil that I had in my pocket. Then, in the white margins, I scribbled hastily, in a disorderly and barely legible fashion. Sr. M. Gabriella knew how to find for each person a word "ad hoc" so that one could say it was inspired! It was especially so when I heard what she said to a novice who was very stubborn in her own "good" ideas: "For me, when the superiors say something, *it would be impossible for me to think differently*." Inside of me, I had a deep feeling, full of admiration: "Ah, holiness is just this!" I remember that time with the same vivid impression. Notice the word *think* and consider it in the context of her very strong personality, her former stubbornness, and her fastidiousness.

The Offering: You ask me if the holocaust of one's very life is a Cistercian tradition. I believe it is a need for every generous soul, especially those in the cloister. We have nothing else but ourselves; we have given everything. By our vows we gave ourselves in the normal way; now we would like to place a greater emphasis on the offering, adding to it a meaning of suffering, consumption, and the renunciation of life, with the acceptance of a premature death.

Published works: The two most notable, the only complete ones, are the biographies published by Morcelliana and the Edizioni Paoline.[6] A student of Propaganda Fide, who had come to visit the tomb, perhaps in 1942, published a short

---

[6] Maria Giovanna Dore, *Suor Maria Gabriella della Trappa di Grottaferrata: Amore e sacrificio per l'unità cristiana* (Rome: Edizioni Paoline, 1940).

biography in "Magyar," the Bohemian language. In Italian, another short biography, *La Sorellina che chiama* (The Little Sister Calling), was written by a well-known author. In America, four or five years ago, a biography was composed from the two Italian biographies, entitled *That All May be One*, by another well-known writer, Madame Williamson, a Religious of the Cenacle.[7] But I do not think it had a great a success, as on the contrary happened in Italy.

Dates mentioned incorrectly: Yes, and it's my fault for not having carefully observed the dates.

It seems to me that, when I received the invitation brochure for the great Octave from the good Father Couturier in December 1937, in preparation for the Octave of January 1938, I wrote a letter, a long letter, dated December 1937. I remember very well the night when I wrote it. Although I was very tired, I did so to please the father, and it was as if driven by force, because I do not naturally like writing letters. The invitation was nothing extraordinary: it is certain that only the one received in 1938 for January 1939 made mention of Mother Immacolata—and at that moment the life of Mother Gabriella was already declining. Perhaps the author had seen the date "1938," without thinking that it was referring to the following January.

What is certain is that Sr. M. Gabriella asked to offer her life in January 1938. I remember the conversation I had with her. But then I didn't pay any attention to it at all, because, as I said above, such a "case" was not uncommon. But experience teaches the superior the need to extinguish these fires that are often ephemeral, because it is rare to find souls—balanced and consistent in what they promise. Precisely for this reason I responded coldly, looking bored (I did it on purpose!), saying, "I am not saying either yes or no; offer it to the will of God." I thought it could be just a flame of straw, but I did not yet know this young nun. Her depth and exceptional willpower

---

[7] Mary Paula Williamson, *That All May be One . . . Ut omnes unum sint* (New York: P. J. Kenedy and Sons, 1949).

proved itself only afterwards. I also remember that I had forgotten the whole incident, and that it was only at the beginning of her illness that I had to ask her, "But wasn't it you who asked me to offer your life, during the Octave for Unity?" Then I remembered it very clearly.

Hospital: I am very sorry not to be able to satisfy you. We didn't do any research; we dropped everything, because prudence required it. I was of the opinion that God would guide everything himself, in spite of me, so I pulled back somewhat. I had to keep the appropriate balance between pressure from both inside and outside, and our superiors in the Order were unhappy about the story of the fragrances, and they were quite against it.

All this would have already come to the surface four years ago—if I'm not mistaken—if the diocesan process had begun, because the auxiliary bishop of Frascati, urged by the bishop of Nuoro, had given permission for it.

Instead nothing has been done: our Order doesn't hurry much. It takes miracles or a push to come from the outside.

For this same reason, namely that one couldn't foresee the future, I have no record or memory of my letters to Sr. Maria Gabriella, who could have torn them up herself on her return from the hospital. Only in one case, due to Providence, I kept hers, but one or several have been lost. I used to keep the letters of the current year, and even older ones according to the time available to me, in order to review them and keep only the important ones. I remember trying to find them in the large pile that awaited sorting, and by that time I doubted finding them.

We kept her clothes and her linens separate. And you know where we got the idea to do this? From our separated brethren at Nashdom Abbey! But at that time we already had the scents of alarm: so I was quick to listen to them, happy in this not to follow only my personal desire.

Photographic material: I will write to Grottaferrata unless you go there to please her. If you go, you can ask for what you want.

In the Morcelliana edition, all that you will find in quotes are notes taken by me when I could and what I remembered after talks I had with my sick daughter. Or I wrote them specifically for the novice at the time, Miss Maria Giovanna, who asked for the notes and then quoted them verbatim.

Maria Giovanna Dore: She had to leave for health reasons to recover her strength in Sardinia after finishing the biography for Paoline Publications. Her bishop did not allow her to leave there. He asked her to start a Benedictine monastery in Olzai, her own village. Her father was a deputy at that time and lived in Rome. Later on, Miss M. Giovanna Dore restored the old monastery of San Magno, not far from Rome, and made a foundation on the island of Ceylon.

She calls this new small branch of the Order "The Benedictines of Unity."

She was extremely intelligent and a holy soul.

Short biography published by Edizioni Paoline. I will transcribe the passages that can be used to trace a moral portrait. But first I want to tell you that in fact it is not rare to find people naturally very well balanced and extremely independent before their "vocation," who afterwards become humble in spirit and sweet. This is because they live under the impulse of the love and the fidelity that God requires, which he rewards with infinitely great graces.

Msgr. Gay writes (I quote roughly), "Often to gain a small seed, God will waste a whole harvest." Think, then, what he does in a faithful soul, who wants and asks only for love.

Mother M. Gabriella belongs to the number of these souls. Each monastery has a few of these "favored souls," but often, almost always, it is the secret of God (and of the superior).

Every so often God takes one in his hand and raises it like a banner.

Page 35.[8] The Reverend Mother compared her to a virgin land, drinking in the first rain and allowing it to penetrate.

---

[8] Page numbers here and below refer to Dore's biography of S. Gabriella, cited above in n. 5 and mentioned by M. Pia as a "short biography published

Page 37. Once she was not easily satisfied, but now all goes well for her, because she finds in everything a hidden reality: Jesus.

Page 39. This page *very true*. Especially her gesture of bringing her hand to her chest (as in the *mea culpa* of the *confiteor*) was frequent, but ever so genuine, so simple, so charming, that it left us spellbound.

Page 44. This is also very true. Although maternal, in the beginning I was afraid that her love for me would become too strong (at the time I was about forty-two years old). I wanted this flower, so straight from the stem, not to bend the slightest bit more than necessary toward the hand that cultivated it. After her return from the hospital, I was sure of her, and our relationship became very intimate on a spiritual level.

Page 53. It's inaccurate. There is talk of February 1937—no, it's January. Note. In this regard, I would add that the article in the July *Unitas* contains many inaccuracies. Among other things: "Mother Immacolata received Extreme Unction in the Chapter Room." No. In the Chapter Room she was given first aid and was taken down to the room that she occupied, and it is there that she received Extreme Unction.

Page 79. Sr. Maria Gabriella suffered visibly for her mistakes in the ceremonies, or singing in the choir. In her relations with the novitiate or the community she put into practice, without even complaining for a moment, her deep conviction: "I don't count, I do nothing." In her own eyes, she was always the last, a very small entity. Her smile had become natural: she was always smiling. She was affectionate like a child with the abbess and mistress, and she humbly marveled at their solicitude for her. She wanted no one to see her or look after her. The passion for being disregarded was something very important for her, walking a step at a time, without wishing to follow the more difficult roads, but allowing herself to be guided. She had a thirst for oblivion and sacrifice—a continuous thirst. She

---

by Edizioni Paoline," to which she refers in response to Gaston Zananiri's questions.

had no demands: everything seemed free, unmerited, and priceless. She lived on gratitude (page 81). Her "thank you" was like the breath of her soul. In her rare relations with those who were in charge of her, she did not ask for anything more than to help her "to love more and more."

Page 83. Holiness was not at all a chimeric idea or something difficult, but something very intelligent, clear, and easy. She wanted to sanctify herself by the perfect fulfillment of her duties.

Page 126. "Thank you—thank you—." The gratitude in which she always lived expanded like an ocean into which her soul plunged and drowned. And she was never to leave it. On her lips, the words expressing this gratitude were invariably simple and modest but had the quality of the depth that animated her.

Page 130. The community, which was completely unaware of the offering she had made, wanted at all costs to maintain and heal this young nun of twenty-three years, who had never made demands on anyone. She had never caused a groan, a disagreement, or a clash; she had never made an "observation" or lacked in delicacy or humility, even with a gesture; she lavished her bright smile on all, without excluding anyone,

Page 135, at the bottom (about Mother Michela). "But she would not enter into a race for zeal and mystical flights for anything in the world. She was even reluctant to admit that such flights were to be desired.—She kept walking by staying under the wings of faith, grateful for what she had received, in love of the goodness of Jesus-God. She gave—without an excess of enthusiasm and inexhaustible in quiet admiration."

Page 136. "We have done nothing for the good of the monastery, but we would suffer until the end of the world, and even more, isn't it true, Sr. Maria Gabriella?" The other replied, calmly: "Yes." She did everything with the consent of the Mother Abbess, offering herself for Unity. She judged herself as the most inept in the house; she could have left without regrets, or harming anyone. She wanted neither to live, nor to die. "As the Lord wishes."

She did not devour or burn her way along but was patient in waiting for the end; she finished step by step, always without heroic appearances.

The Lord himself in coming to meet her would set a fire to the path that separated them.

Note to page 141. "She was averse to making herself known." She even eagerly wanted to be forgotten, left aside, and she did nothing to attract attention for the sake of making sure that we looked after her. One had to question her in order for her to talk about herself. This modesty sprang from her love: she wanted to be entirely for Jesus, to be his alone. She had to be entirely free for him, to do anything he wanted. She kept herself jealously for him. It is I who tell you all this, wasting many words—but in all this she was extremely simple, not so much naturally, but with a simplicity that was thought out and willed.

Page 141. I return to page 141, and I copy: "She did not have any direct correspondence with the separated brethren. Thus, her offering was entirely between herself and God, and it was expressed only in suffering. The offering was not made in a written document, as usually happens, and she never felt the need to talk about it. Even when it was necessary to say how and why she was sick, to her mother and to the good confessor, for some time it was the Mother Abbess who had to take this assignment upon herself."

(I don't quite remember if I mentioned this to her mother; to her confessor, maybe, but I do not know.)

"Sister Maria Gabriella was as jealous of her charity as of her virginity: she had the same lily-like modesty."

Page 142. One cannot think of an interior life simpler than hers. No ascetic feats, nor did she make efforts to place herself in this or that degree of prayer; no baggage of devotions (supplementary prayers), nor of practical additions to the Mass and the Divine Office.

Note: She used to say the rosary and was very fond of the Stations of the Cross, which were placed in the corridor of the infirmary. In all things she has her place among the great ascetic figures and mystical personages of her Order, the Order of Cîteaux, and the Trappists in particular. The monastery for her was simply Jesus, his love, his will, and his glory. She was his disciple and his bride, imitating the Blessed Virgin Mary, who welcomed Jesus in her womb, responding to the Angel of the Annunciation: "*Ecce . . . fiat mihi.*"

Note: I wrote, "The Order of La Trappe," because here where I am (La Fille-Dieu, at Romont) they don't like the very popular name of "Trappist." They prefer the real name of the beginning of the Order, "Cistercian." In fact the Order is officially called "The Order of Cistercians of the Strict Observance. O.C.S.O."

Note Page 144. Her prayer. (A vision of a crucifix on two red carpets.) It happened just like that, so there was something mysterious.

Page 160. Remarkable and characteristic of her answer to my question if she didn't have anything to say to the community. Failure in the Usages for giving thanks and asking for forgiveness. But Sr. M. Gabriella was too young in the religious life and could not know this Usage.

Note about her, "What should I say?" It is the embarrassment of a person who does not think about herself. And then her two dominant sentiments: gratitude and humility, summarized in four words: "Ringrazio tanto e mi perdonino."[9]

Biography published by Morcelliana[10]

Page 16. The foreword is by Giordani, a holy man, simple and humble, a combative apologist, and a representative in Parliament. "I'm here for the love of God and of his Church. . . ." It's a beautiful passage: you can take all you wish from Giordani's preface because he is a man who is above all pettiness.

---

[9] "Thank you so much, and forgive me."
[10] See n. 5 above.

". . . those offered to love and to the passion of Christ, for the glory of his name and the benefit of the souls redeemed by Him . . . do not get distracted or waste time. At every moment, they pour out tears and prayers, vigils, and fasts into the common Treasury of the Church, for persons far away who will benefit and who on earth will not know, maybe ever, by whom they were raised up. And so their houses are centers of unending reconstruction of spiritual health for everyone, and their people are raised up as victims of atonement, between the negligences of the children and the justice of the Father: they are anvils like Catherine, their sister, by whom God's wrath is broken."[11]

Page 17. "It demands a total and absolute love. It is essential to practice piety, without detours and without compromise. Above all, without weaknesses."

Preface: from page 19 to 20. A very nice summary of the biography, from "The book narrates . . ." to the second paragraph of page 20.

Note: I think it would be good to quote this page or at least to take the ideas. Note the words, *Sister Maria Gabriella is the sister who takes you by the hand*. These words have been very successful. In Italian *sorellina*[12] is not used like the French *petite soeur* or *petites soeurs*, which is also the name of some religious institutions. In this case there is something very distinct and characteristic.

Page 40. Here we find her usual habit of gratitude, thanksgiving, and praise.

Page 42. This page is very true. It took Sr. M. Gabriella two months to conquer her faults of impatience, being demanding, critical, and stubborn. I remember well her confession. This proves her strong will power. Because in fact, when she entered the monastery, the terrain of her soul was already well cleared; she soaked up the instructions she received (mainly because she had a memory that helped her a lot), so much so that I

---

[11] Unspecified, but presumably Catherine of Siena
[12] Little sister

marveled at her wisdom, which she learned from the experience of others. Her humble docility of spirit, common sense, and loyalty to grace led her in three and a half years of monastic life to the heights (of virtue).

The sense of justice and truth was very pronounced in her. I remember that during a singing practice in the novitiate, I asked for an explanation about a small incident that had happened for which I have completely forgotten the reason. A novice gave her explanation, and Sr. M. Gabriella specified everything with a clarity, a steadiness, a "justice" that struck me, and which I still remember very well with the thought that I had at that moment: "here's one who won't tolerate anything ambiguous!"

Page 63. This page is very true.

Page 74. At the bottom of the page: moral portrait of Mother Immacolata. Very nice.

Page 79. Second subsection, in the middle of the page. I can only repeat what I wrote then.

Page 82. The bottom of the page reveals her aim: the glory of God. Her good sense and her pure heart internalized the core of the teachings she received, the most important point, the center.

The "common" of Virgins (the majority of women religious) does not come so quickly—far from it!

Sr. Gabriella's coherence helped her a lot with this.

Only he—Only God—therefore "not I."

Nothing about me; otherwise, we would be two.

Page 87. The second paragraph from the bottom of the page is a passage exposing a very true moral portrait: *Ecce . . . fiat mihi*. Readiness and absence of personal self will.

Here also her consistency stands out: God, who knows everything and can do everything, brought her to surrender herself completely to him. Her concern was only to be faithful to him. Towards the end of her life, she speaks with a novice: "What, would we like to give advice to Jesus?"

Pages 89 and 90, at the bottom of the page. Here's the answer to your question on how the offering came about: it was like that.

Page 93. It was the only resistance on her part that I remember.[13]

Note. She was shocked: she no longer had the physical strength to get up. I remember that, as the signal for work had already been given, I had to get away quickly to oversee its distribution. I left her there thunderstruck, with her hands extended toward me. Evidently it was a blow, though in itself, there was no reason to be so upset. But what hurt her most deeply was this: what she had done to displease Jesus by insisting on her own idea.

Page 94. Towards the middle of the page—up until page 95, there is a beautiful accent on Unity.

Page 120. Second paragraph—Moral portrait. Very good.

I remember hearing from someone that at the hospital they pointed out the place facing the crucifix in the room where Sr. M. Gabriella had been, and said, "There was a young Trappist sister here."

Page 126. Last paragraph: very true, in speaking of her delicacy to avoid infection.

Page 134. This history of the five lire embarrassed a monk who translated the biography into Dutch. It seemed to be a case of a "mistaken conscience." I had to write an explanation: 5 lire then (7–8 Swiss francs today [in 1953!]) was approximately the salary for a working day. A deficiency contrary to the vow of poverty was beginning there, and sometimes the virtue of poverty is injured with something very small.

Page 135. Calling it "grave sin" evidently caused confusion. In fact, the nurse, her fellow Sardinian and novitiate companion, a holy soul—who died of a cancer last December—paid it no heed.

It is an experience that I had personally and also with other sisters: that is how one becomes sensitive on the subject of

---

[13] The impression she had of having done poorly at her turn as *invitatrix*. Note of Augusta Tescari, OCSO, who translated the *Réponses* from French to Italian. Henceforth in these footnotes *translator* will indicate this first phase of the translation.

poverty in the religious life, especially in the beginning. We feel we have received gratuitously even if we bring a significant dowry, so we love the house, and therefore if we cause any damage, even if minimal, it is unbearable. On the other hand, the vow of poverty is the one that we sense more than the others, whose matter is more moral.

Note on the smile of Sr. Gabriella.

It was Mother Michela who reminded me of this after the death of Sister Gabriella. In the first days after her arrival, especially when doing the laundry, she expressed exuberant gaiety. She had bursts of laughter, not loud, but frequent. It was the joy of being where she belonged, where God wanted her. This joy is something that generally occurs even today.[14] By nature she was quite pensive without being sad or gloomy—oh no!—but she was sensitive to the merriment of the environment. I do not know if she received any criticism about the frequent laughter, or if there was a general rebuke about such in the novitiate, as happens when you do not want to cause pain,[15] but the fact is that I remember Sr. M. Gabriella became very serious and that the smile which was an appropriate gesture—acquired for virtue—after the reprimand received about her attitude was sometimes too serious and grim.

Page 175. Another inaccuracy. Every Cistercian monastery should have its own cemetery within the enclosure. At Grotta we couldn't have one because the property was too small to allow a proper site for the cemetery, a free area of a radius at least two hundred meters as required by hygienic law in Italy.

However our crypt—very beautiful—was separated from the crypt tombs of the parish only by means of a wall (it was the tomb of the family of those who had built the parish church). And there was even a very decent room, contiguous to this family tomb and separate from the crypt by means of

---

[14] Among postulants [translator's note]
[15] To an individual [translator's note]

a wall. I wanted very much to get permission to transform this room into a tomb, crypt tombs for the community, especially as our common grave in the cemetery was almost full. Mother Immacolata was the last to go out of the enclosure.[16] We prayed. Before Easter we finally got permission for "temporary storage" (which is still valid).[17] I passed by the nurse to give her the news: "We have permission for the tombs." M. Michela and the good, elderly mother, who would die fifteen days before Sr. M. Gabriella, were ecstatic with joy. Sr. Maria Gabriella whispered, calmly, but with eyes beaming, "Now I can die." She was the second to occupy the tomb, and Mother Michela, who departed just three months later—on July 23—was the third.

Clarification: Somewhere in the Italian press, in the articles that were published in large numbers after the biography, it was written that Sr. M. Gabriella had offered herself for the Anglicans. No. God allowed relations with Nashdom Abbey for his purposes and, practically speaking, to give more importance to the history of Sr. Maria Gabriella. But she gave her life for Christ's desire that *all* may be one.

For you. Dom Benedict, a holy monk, came to Grotta in 1947 (verify the dates!), if I'm not mistaken, with a Benedictine oblate of his abbey, sixty-four years old, I believe, who was formerly the Governor of Nigeria, Br. Francis de Sales, who spoke French perfectly. Dom Benedict speaks it quite well. To make you understand the greatness of spirit of Dom Benedict, just how great that soul was, I will quote these words. During his visit, I told him that the doubt about the validity of ordination must be painful for him. He turned pale, and after a moment replied, "If I were certain of not being a priest, I would die of sorrow." They were taken to Castel Gandolfo and granted a small special audience with the Holy Father. Dom Benedict, kneeling before him, said, "I have offered my life for

---

[16] For burial
[17] In 1953

Unity like Sr. Maria Gabriella." Returning from the papal audience they were so excited that they couldn't speak.

Last year the oblate became a Catholic. All this is *for you* and your friends, not for the public.

I remember something. I'm not sure if it happened after the Extreme Unction or after the Communion of Viaticum, but I think it was after the Extreme Unction. With a graceful air, but with authority Sr. M. Gabriella said, "And now, everything goes." And good Sr. Benedetta, the nurse, who had known her in the novitiate (about fifteen years older than Sr. Gabriella, she had entered at thirty-four), in order to please Sr. Gabriella, had to take her clothing away along with some books that were for her personal use.

She wanted to leave poor, bare, with nothing: "everything goes!" I remember this because it made us smile. But we understood.

I do not know if this incident is in the biography: I have not seen it, but it could be that I passed over it without noticing it.

Her struggle to accept death.

It was Donna Maria Giovanna who told me that there had been a battle and that it stood out clearly in the letters.

As for me, I had not noticed it at all. She never expressed regret, didn't ask me to help her in the struggle, and didn't admit any repugnance to me.

However, I remember that I was struck by a phrase that Sr. M. Gabriella uttered, as though talking to herself. Here's the drift of it:

At a certain moment, in the infirmary, the father chaplain spoke to us about a person, "a healer," who cured tuberculosis patients and had done wonders in a sanatorium. Mother Michela, who knew the chagrin I felt and who realized that I would very much miss both herself and Sr. Gabriella, remained for a few days under the influence of this impression, this hope. Then it all fell apart by itself, without the father chaplain speaking about it anymore; it was one of those baseless enthusiasms of public opinion!

But I remember that Sr. M. Gabriella told me something with a strange expression that struck me: "Mother Michela does not say anything more about that . . . she had to resign herself—" and did not finish the phrase. Now recalling what Miss Maria Giovanna said to me, I understand that she intuited in her companion the struggle for life, the battle between desire and repulsion through which she herself had also passed. This is a battle that she overcame alone, with her strong will and the help of grace, to which she was so faithful—.

Her docility, her abandonment came—it seems to me—because she intuited the greatness of God, and, without analyzing her feelings, she lived in the concrete adoration of the God who had chosen her and loved her. She felt so unworthy, so small, so nothing: this stemmed from her humility and gratitude.

This is what I think I understood from rereading the biographies.

The Daily Schedule

I will send you the booklet that is sent from here (La Fille-Dieu) for those who ask for information about our life, called "The Cistercian Abbey of La Fille-Dieu, founded in 1263."

The timetable is written very clearly in this brochure.

✣ ✣ ✣ ✣

I'll send another brochure together with that one, "The Cistercian Religious. . . ."

It is already thirty-five years old, but it might still interest you, because we do not change things very much!

The diet is based on dairy products, vegetables, pasta, and rice, fruit, or jam, as the final dish is served only at noon, except during Lent and Fridays outside Paschal time, or in the evening, during the time of fasting. Everything is taken with bread and the drink of the local region. From Easter to Pentecost, in the evening we have dairy products, cheese or something similar. Eggs are allowed as a supplement for those who need it. Meat or fish is served in the infirmary.

Let me copy for you (because it is practical and because I really like it) this thought of Msgr. Gay in one of his "Elevations":

> *Living in universal love and destroying within us and around us—insofar as possible—all that is opposed to the Union of all people in the One, we fulfill the prayer that Christ made to his Father, and we are linked to the welcome, and to the effectiveness, that the Father gives to his Son.*

Conclusion

Here you are, Dear Sir: that is all I can say. I ask you to excuse the disorder and language. May God help you because you write for him, for the great desire of the heart of his Son. He is himself grateful!

Humbly and with deep gratitude,
Sr. Maria Pia, OCSO

My most respectful homage to Monsignor Dumont.

Mother M. Pia Gullini and Sister Maria Gabriella[1]

The Cistercian tradition, with its spirituality so rich and so steeped in humanity, does not come to us only through texts, but also through history. History is our great teacher. When I speak of history I do not speak of events, but of people, because it is people who make up the historical space in which we move.

How can a community think of the heavenly Jerusalem without thinking to examine the faces of the sisters who have served the earthly Jerusalem in the humble joy of their self-donation?

We are all indebted to the humanity and holiness of those who have gone before us.

Mother Cristiana Piccardo[2]

We know that Maria Sagheddu came to the monastery of Grottaferrata on September 30, 1935. This is how Mother Pia describes her first meeting in the parlor with Maria and her first impressions, according to notes written for Mother Maria Giovanna Dore, the author of the first biography of Sister Maria Gabriella:

---

[1] Previous printings of this article are Maria Paola Santachiara, "Madre M. Pia Gullini e Suor Maria Gabriella," *Vita Nostra* 38, no. 2 (2009): 37–52; and "Mother Maria Pia Gullini and Sister Maria Gabriella," CSQ 47, no. 4 (2012): 407–27.

[2] Cristiana Piccardo, *Pedagogia Viva* (Milan: Jaca Books, 1999), 33–34.

> She arrived on September 30, twenty-one years of age, fine and fresh, with big eyes—deep and bright. Her soul shone pure and full of amazement before the mystery of the House of the Lord, of religious life.
>
> Rev. Mother, after some conversations, realized the depth of this soul, who possessed an uncommon memory, if not to say unique, a broad intelligence, and a tranquil equilibrium.
>
> Humble and childlike in soul, she drank in everything around her, and it permeated her. The life of the Trappists, with its mystery of silence, its prayer of praise, its court-like ceremonies, its penances done with Christ the victim, was all a life of love. It was a conversation with the celestial beings; it was the price of souls, the life of Paradise, but a death to oneself; death, the absolute condition for this angelic life, in the unseen ways and in activity. She grasped it immediately and, with her strong will, embraced the renunciation of herself in order to follow him who is her Lord, and she would later be found worthy to carry his cross.[3]

These are words that already as in seed summarized a whole life and that slowly, in the wake of a loving daily fidelity, would lead to the fulfillment of a vocation of love and offering. For her part, Maria wrote in her first letter to her mother,

> If you knew how good the Reverend Superior is! She seems more a heavenly mother than an earthly one. That's how good her advice and her words are, and the Novice Mistress, with whom I've spoken today, is also very good.
>
> If you heard the choir sisters sing you would say it seems like a great number of angels and not people.
>
> Everything here inspires peace and quiet in me, and I hope, with the help of the Lord, to be just fine. . . . (Letter 1)[4]

---

[3] M. Pia Gullini, "Appunti della Rev. Madre su Suor Maria Gabriella," Archives of Vitorchiano. These "Notes of Rev. Mother on Sr. M. Gabriela" are cited below as Gullini, "Notes."

[4] Sr. Maria Gabriella's Letters are quoted from their translations in this volume.

The immediate result of the first impression made by the postulant from Dorgali was the abbess's free choice, from the first day, to count her among the choir nuns, a decision that filled Gabriella with confusion, thinking of her friends from Dorgali, who were all lay sisters. There was the fear of knowing that she did not have sufficient singing skills for carrying out such a task, but, at the same time, there was gratitude for the undeserved gift of singing the praises of the Lord. She expresses herself in this way when giving the news to Don Meloni:

> He wanted me closer to him because Reverend Mother placed me in the choir for the psalmody and to sing his praises. I should be very grateful and give thanks for this special grace accorded to me, but you can imagine, Reverend Father, how confusing it is for me, who never really understood music and singing. Nevertheless, I do everything possible to study it and hope that Jesus, if he really wants me, will help me. (Letter 4)

To her mother she gave the news a few months later, in these terms:

> My heavenly bridegroom granted me yet another grace. Reverend Mother placed me in the choir to sing his praises day and night, and this grace was given to me not just now, but from the first day that I entered the community.
>
> I knew, however, that I am little adapted for singing, and that's why I have not written anything about it, not knowing how I was going to end up. (Letter 6)[5]

---

[5] Mother Carla Valtorta shares her testimony, showing the extent of the commitment with which Sister Maria Gabriella tried to fulfill her task as a choir nun and her fears, not totally unfounded, of not being able to live up to it. Mother Carla writes, "After the little office of Our Lady and meditation, at 2:30 a.m., we started to sing the Canonical Office. Sister Maria Gabriella, who was the *invitatrix* that week, went to the middle of the choir to sing the invitatory with the help of another sister a bit more talented than she was. The harmonium had given the first note, but Sister Maria Gabriella didn't

Mother Pia then describes Gabriella's physical appearance in answer to some questions of Gaston Zananiri,[6] the author of the first French biography of Gabriella:

> She was beautiful, but her modesty hid her like a veil, even before entering . . .
> Her stature was slightly above average. . . . Broad forehead and beautiful, bright large eyes with a deep expression and so transparent that when she came to see me, I had the impression of seeing her soul. . . .
> Her mouth was rather large, but her smile had a sweetness, a stunning beauty that revealed her teeth, white and straight, which manifested youth and health. The chin was broad and very strong-willed. Hers was a classic profile.[7]

If we continue to read some of these answers we can detect their psychological subtlety in the study of the personality of Sister Maria Gabriella and the maternal love with which Mother Pia accompanied this daughter of election by collaborating with the grace of the Lord, not seeking anything other than to help her to love Jesus more and more with her whole being. We read in the memories of Mother Carla:

---

catch it correctly; her partner gave the note in a strong voice in order to bring her to a higher note, but Sister Gabriella, believing it to be an encouragement to sing louder, sang out louder. It was a solemn dissonance to the end. When we arrived at the *"Gloria Patri,"* she took a breath. In my heart I said, "God was glorified just the same." It should have been very discouraging for the poor little *invitatrix*, but no, I saw her back in her stall with her head down as usual, looking confused, but smiling and calm. When intoning the antiphons for the third nocturne and for Lauds, which were rather difficult because of the beautiful melody so rich in notes, she didn't lose courage, and she motioned to her neighbor to help her. It was a surprise for all to hear two voices instead of one, but it went well. For her, the important thing was that the praises of God should go well, with fervor and dignity" (M. Maria Carla Valtorta, "Presentation on the Virtues of Sr. Maria Gabriella Sagheddu," Archives of Vitorchiano).

[6] Gaston Zananiri, *Dans le Mystère de l'Unité: Maria Gabriella* (Paris, Tournai: Casterman, 1955).

[7] M. Pia Gullani, "Autograph Notebooks of M. Pia Gullini: Responses to Gaston Zananiri's Questions," Vitorchiano Archives, 1953; p. 146 above.

Rev. Mother Pia confided to me that when Sister Maria Gabriella appeared for the individual interview it was always brief, but before leaving, with her head down and flushed from shyness, when asking the blessing she said, "Thank you, Reverend Mother; help me to love Jesus more and more.[8]

And so Mother Pia writes in her réponses to Zananiri:

> She said hardly anything, but her total gift, her docility, absolute and deliberate, her calm personal equilibrium, humble gratitude, and affection, pure and filial: all this you could read in her eyes. And it could be read so well, that I myself could not find anything to say, or very little.
>
> . . . In this regard I remember that while I was making the annual retreat at the end of October 1938, a time when the superior does not speak to the community, I saw her go into the choir for the visit to the Blessed Sacrament, while the community was at work. I remembered that day, October 31, the eve of All Saints' Day, and in 1937 it was the feast of Christ the King, so it was the anniversary of her profession. There was a custom for the young nuns who wanted to, to go to Reverend Mother on the anniversary of their profession and renew their vows. The little one (Sr. Gabriella) had been in the infirmary for five months. Reverend Mother called her and went out, motioning her to follow her. Sister Maria Gabriella was glad. She repeated the formula of the vows with her hands in the hands of the abbess; she received the ritual embrace with the answer: "God reward thee with everlasting life." She didn't say a word, but her beautiful bright eyes and her wonderfully charming smile expressed her joy and gratitude. Mother looked for a holy card and gave it to her, without herself saying a word, either, and watched her walk away, so simple, humble, and yet dignified. She was astonished and edified by this silence, which caused her to admire once

---

[8] Valtorta, "Presentation on the Virtues."

again the deep Cistercian spirit that revealed itself more with actions than with words.⁹

Various testimonies speak of some initial severity of the Reverend Mother toward Gabriella. Mother Pia herself gives us confirmation of that in her Notes:

> By an instinct that surprised herself, Rev. Mother was almost always strict with her, trying to mold that exquisitely feminine soul straight towards heaven, straight and strong, and quickly. It was demanding; pushing towards the heights, she was unaware of the unshakeable will disguised under that sensibility. She knew her only after her great trial in the hospital. Then Reverend Mother bent towards that flower with devotion, with respect, and with holy fear enfolded in a supernatural affection; then mother and daughter understood one another.[10]

And also from M. Dore: "Without letting her understand her intuitive tenderness, indeed treating her a little sternly, Mother considered Sister M. Gabriella as an alabaster vase that the Lord had brought there so that all its perfume would be poured onto his feet."[11]

In response to Zananiri M. Pia explains the reason for her initial severity:

> Although maternal, in the beginning I was afraid that her love for me would become too strong (at the time I was about forty-two years old). I wanted this flower, so straight from the stem, not to bend the slightest bit more than necessary toward the hand that cultivated it. After her return

---

⁹ Gullini, "Notebooks," p. 147. M. Pia refers to herself in the third person here and in subsequent passages.

¹⁰ Gullini, "Notes."

¹¹ Maria Giovanna Dore, *Amore e sacrificio per l'Unità della Chiesa. Suor Maria Gabriella della Trappa di Grottaferrata* (Rome: Pia Società S. Paolo, 1940), 35.

from the hospital, I was sure of her, and our relationship became very intimate on a spiritual level.[12]

Unfortunately, the letters written by Mother Pia during Sister Gabriella's hospital stay were lost.[13] But looking at those from Sister Maria Gabriella to Mother Pia, we see how the correspondence between them became frequent, confidential, marked by a crescendo of filial affection and of loving trust and gratitude, even in suffering and the struggle for obedience to what was being asked.

The "Reverend Mother" written at the heading of Gabriella's first letter from the hospital (Letter 27, April 19, 1938), was increasingly replaced in subsequent letters by "Dearest Reverend Mother." Let us take a quick glance at each letter. We will not repeat the many beautiful phrases in this correspondence, which might be considered a masterpiece of simple and profound spirituality, but stick to those that concern us in this context:

> Thank you very much for all that you've written and sent. . . . Pray for me, because I have so much need of prayer. Sometimes I wonder if the Lord has not abandoned me; other times I think he tries those whom he loves, and yet at other times it seems impossible that God can be glorified by this sort of life; but I always end up abandoning myself to the divine will.
> I greet you with all my heart, and I ask you to bless me. (Letter 29, April 24, 1938)

> Thank you for your letter and the prayers that you and the others offer for me. I feel their effect because these days are a bit quieter. Everything seems easy when we are at

---

[12] Gullini, "Notebooks," p. 155.
[13] Mother M. Pia attests, "I have no record or memory of my letters to Sr. Maria Gabriella, who could have torn them up herself on her return from the hospital. Only in one case, due to Providence, I kept hers, but one or several have been lost" (Gullini, "Notebooks," p. 153).

peace, but when the Lord tries us, we realize our weakness. I have offered myself entirely to my Jesus, and I do not take back my word. I am weak, it is true, but the Lord knows my frailty and the cause of my pain. He forgives me, and I am convinced of this. . . .

Reverend Mother, I wish you a happy feast day and all that your heart desires. I haven't been able to do anything for you, but I offer my prayers, my communions, and my sacrifices to the Lord for your intention to be sanctified more and more. He has permitted that this year I cannot participate in your feast day. *Fiat*. . . .

. . . We will find ourselves this day in the Heart of Jesus. (Letter 30, April 28, 1938)

Yesterday the good Father Chaplain came to see me and brought me your dear letter. Thank you very much for what you have done for me, and please thank all the people who are concerned about me. May the Lord reward you all abundantly in heaven. I am very sorry that I displeased you with my letter. I don't want to apologize so many times, but only ask forgiveness with all my heart. . . .

. . . Pray for me, that I will increasingly understand the great gift of the cross and that from now on it will benefit me and all the others.

I feel that now you love me more and that also my heart increases in my love for you. In this regard I suffered a lot both from the devil, who tempted me to judge my superiors as heartless for leaving me here, and also from other people who make the same accusation. I certainly did not hesitate to drive out these temptations, and I assure you that I won. I say this with filial simplicity, and if I could show you my heart like an open book, I would be happy to do so.

The Lord keeps me naked on the cross, and I have no other consolation than to know that I suffer in order to fulfill God's will in a spirit of obedience. . . .

. . . I do not know if it will be convenient to change my room again, but as the Lord gives you the grace to see further than I can, Reverend Mother, do what you think is best. . . .

. . . Tomorrow and the day after I will offer my day for you, praying to the Lord to bless and sanctify you more and more so that you can sanctify the others. I commend myself to your prayers, in which I put all my hope.

I greet you with the most filial affection, and I embrace you wholeheartedly.

> Your daughter,
> Sister Maria Gabriella (Letter 31, May 3, 1938)

Yesterday I received your package and your letter, and I thank you for everything. I understand your decision about my return; I know you do everything for my greater good, but I don't hide the fact that this was painful for me. . . .

Always your daughter, who only wants to return to your embrace,

> Sister Maria Gabriella (Letter 32, May 10, 1938)

Thank you very much for your dear letter and for what you sent me, which I received this morning. Thank you for your good words and good advice.

For a long time I have been convinced that I am only a pygmy in the way of the spirit, because I get carried about with every wind that blows. My soul is here like one lost, because it doesn't have its mother (the abbess) or a friend whom it can ask for advice when it feels the need. . . .

My dear Mother, pray much that I don't lose my religious spirit. That's my one great fear, my biggest fear, because I feel so weak and able to fall at any moment.

The Lord will help me, because he never abandons those who put all their confidence in him. I also expect the help of your prayers. (Letter 33, May 22, 1938)

Concerning this last letter, Mother M. Carla writes in her "Report,"

> In the Trappist monasteries when speaking with the first Superior, we always say "My Reverend Mother." Sister

Maria Gabriella, lying in the hospital, adhered to this respectful rule when she wrote to her superior. Although she began her letters "Dearest Reverend Mother," the tone is always respectful. Only in one letter from the hospital, and as though a bit lost, the poor girl turns to her Superior calling her "Mother." The Rev. Mother Pia said to me: "I have never been called 'Mother' from anyone, but being called 'Mother' by this dear child, I felt great joy."[14]

We read in the Prologue of the Rule of Saint Benedict,

> Listen, my son, to your master's precepts, and incline the ear of your heart. Receive willingly and carry out effectively your loving father's advice, that by the labor of obedience you may return to Him from whom you had departed by the sloth of disobedience. To you, therefore, my words are now addressed, whoever you may be, who are renouncing your own will to do battle under the Lord Christ, the true King, and are taking up the strong, bright weapons of obedience. . . .
>
> And so we are going to establish a school for the service of the Lord. In founding it we hope to introduce nothing harsh or burdensome. But if a certain strictness results from the dictates of equity for the amendment of vices or the preservation of charity, do not be at once dismayed and fly from the way of salvation, whose entrance cannot but be narrow. For as we advance in the religious life and in faith our hearts expand and we run the way of God's commandments with unspeakable sweetness of love. Thus, never departing from His school, but persevering in the monastery according to his teaching until death, we may by patience share in the sufferings of Christ and deserve to have a share also in His kingdom.[15]

---

[14] M. Carla Valtorta, "Presentation on the Virtues," 18.
[15] *Saint Benedict's Rule for Monasteries*, trans. Leonard Doyle (Collegeville, MN: Liturgical Press, 1948), 1.5–6.

It was in this school of divine service that Gabriella grew. It was a demanding school of total and undivided love for the Lord, whom she loved with her whole being in the good times and the bad, a filial and spousal adherence to his will, loved and lived at all times and in all circumstances.

[The Environment at Grottaferrata; the Ministry of Dom Norbert Sauvage, OCSO][16]

Here the reader is referred to two excellent articles by Mother Augusta Tescari on Mother Pia[17] in which Sister M. Marta Morganti, biographer of Mother Dore, is quoted describing Dore as a "shaper of monastic consciences."[18] I think it is appropriate to say the same thing about Mother Pia herself, about the environment that Maria Sagheddu found on entering Grottaferrata, and about her mother mistress, Mother Tecla.[19] These were the people and environment that helped her to fulfill her desire for total surrender to Jesus Christ, initially forged from the beginning of her conversion in Dorgali with her collaboration with the Lord's grace under the enlightened and paternal spiritual guidance of Don Basilio Meloni.[20] Father

---

[16] Bracketed headers in this article are provided by its translator.

[17] On Mother Pia, see Augusta Tescari, "Madre Pia Gullini, fervente promotrice per l'unità dei cristiani," *L'Osservatore Romano*, 4 July 1999, 5; Augusta Tescari, "Una grande badessa del XX secolo: Madre Pia Gullini," *L'Ulivo, Rivista olivetana di spiritualità e di cultura monastica* 2 (2006): 3–31.

[18] M. Marta Morganti, *Maria Giovanna Dore* (Brescia: Morcelliana, 2001), 189.

[19] Mother Tecla Fontana, born in Milan on April 24, 1871, in 1888 entered the Congregation of the Franciscan Missionaries of Egypt and departed immediately for Cairo. She returned to Rome in 1913 and entered Grottaferrata January 20, 1917. Not accepted for profession, she left in July 1919 and entered the monastery of Chimay in Belgium. Requested by Mother M. Pia to be mistress of novices, on April 20, 1932, she went to Grotta, where she made her stability on January 20, 1935. She was elected as abbess of the community for two terms, from 1940 to 1946, and as superior *ad nutum* in 1951–1952. She died on November 10, 1955.

[20] Don (Father) Basilio Meloni (1900–1967): assistant pastor in Dorgali from 1925 to 1927 and from 1930 to 1935, and pastor from 1939 to 1967.

Meloni testified at the process for beatification: "She let herself be guided completely and obediently by me, her spiritual director, and made steady progress in virtue."[21]

The community of Grotta, as well as both Mother Pia and Mother Tecla, owed their monastic formation to Dom Norbert Sauvage, the former abbot of Scourmont, Belgium, who was the Trappist procurator general in Rome from 1913 until the year of his death, which took place at the Order's Generalate.[22] From the beginning of his stay in Rome, Dom Norbert took charge of the spiritual formation of the community of Grottaferrata; he was also their confessor for some years. On the afternoon of each Saturday and the eve of holidays he used to go to Grottaferrata, staying there until the following day, hearing confessions and giving lectures. He wanted the nuns to be formed in a solid spirituality, that is to say, in the Scriptures and the sources of Cistercian spirituality. He gave special courses to the novices, who also attended those of the whole community.[23]

We read in the diary of Mother Teresa Bottasso,[24]

> It is 1914 and we are in the Great War. We were fortunate to have Dom Norbert as chaplain. The first time I went to confession to Dom Norbert, I felt a great repugnance to confess, but at his first words I was comforted. He under-

---

[21] *Positio super virtutibus* 156.

[22] Dom Norbert Sauvage was born on July 3, 1876, at Avesnes-le-Sec, France. On September 4, 1894, he entered the Trappist monastery of Scourmont in Belgium. Elected abbot of the community on January 15, 1902, he resigned in October 1913. He was then sent to Rome as procurator of the Trappist Order. He died in Rome on July 8, 1923, and is buried in the cemetery of the Abbey of the Tre Fontane.

[23] Armand Veilleux, "Dom Norbert Sauvage: L'art de préparer son successeur," *Collectanea Cisterciensia* 63 (2001): 213–23.

[24] Mother Teresa Bottasso was born in Peveragno, in Cuneo, on January 8, 1881. On September 8, 1896, she entered St. Vito, in Turin. She made perpetual profession on November 13, 1900, and died at Vitorchiano on August 9, 1965, the last one of the nuns who had entered at St. Vito.

stood my good intentions and put his hand to work at tearing out the weeds. I believe that he prayed for me, and what a saint he was, immediately putting his finger on the wound and not saying the same thing twice. With him you had to walk without stopping. With such a director, deficiencies disappeared, and one had to run, or rather to fly, in the way of perfection.[25]

[Mother Teresa's Diary]: [Feast of the] Sacred Heart, June 7, 1918

> Following the teachings and the direction of my spiritual father I will make the greatest efforts to acquire true humility; to take the occasions of repressing pride I'll try to accept not being not included, being put aside, forgotten, misunderstood, crushed, and trampled upon. When humiliated, I will be silent, without a lot of explanations, and promptly kneeling I will say "mea culpa."[26]

Here is the transcript of a note of Dom Norbert to Mother Teresa:

> Rome, April 3, 1919
>
> You don't bother me at all; I am pleased to give peace to your soul and a boost in the service of Jesus. You should practice humility generously, and not in an ordinary way, but profoundly; mortification not in an ordinary way, but at every moment. This is the condition demanded by Jesus to continue his divine work in your soul. Moreover, you must live with Jesus, recollected and detached. Jesus wishes to guide you, but then you must take him by the hand, or at least return to him often during the day. The action of Jesus in you depends on fidelity to the practice of humility, mortification, and union with him. Be faithful

---

[25] "Diary of Mother Teresa Bottasso," unpublished manuscript, 16.
[26] Bottasso, "Diary," 31.

and generous; that is so important for you! Oh! If only you understood this you would be afraid of being negligent, of not responding well to this precious action of Jesus in your soul. In the virtues, especially humility, you must try to be more perfect. In sacrifices you must never spare yourself, and Jesus will not put any limit to his graces of election for poor Teresa.

Brother Norbert[27]

Thanks to Mother Tecla Fontana, some excerpts of conferences given by Dom Norbert at Grotta are preserved in the archives of Scourmont. M. Tecla wrote, "I believe that what is presented is passages from various conferences (plural) given by Dom Norbert. M. Tecla." Let us look at some passages.

Formation of the Interior Life

The love of the heart of Jesus is an abyss, an ocean that the soul must continually savor, especially the soul of those espoused to Jesus, of contemplative religious. What we are interested to know in Jesus is his love, his heart. . . .

In order to study his heart we have to study and meditate on the whole Gospel to discover all the love he shows us. . . . This study of Jesus, we will learn, reveals especially his heart. We don't know Jesus when we don't know his heart and when we don't feel caught up by the love that the divine heart shows us. But for us, now, the real Jesus of the earth is the eucharistic Jesus. Then, after having studied him in the Gospel, we must study him in the Eucharist. . . .

Would that every day your soul would progress through prayer in the knowledge of the love of Jesus. Then love will become easier for you. I do not speak of a sentimental love, but an enlightened and reasonable love that will support you in service of a constant and generous love,

---

[27] Bottasso, "Diary," 32.

despite all the dryness and difficulties that you may encounter. . . .

How much our Cistercian life requires enthusiasm and holy joy! Now the point of the strict regulations, the austere observance, and numerous exercises is not to tire the body and spirit . . . they will, in fact, have this effect, but the point is rather to lead us to the love of Jesus. Therefore we must leave meditation every morning filled with Jesus, and not cease to work to acquire perfect love. For those who are often troubled, restless, and oppressed by scruples, rather than making many examinations of conscience that are disturbing, it would be better for them to meditate on the many beautiful scenes of the Gospel where Jesus reveals his merciful heart. . . .

Let us ask the holy Virgin to give us her horror of pride in all its forms. One might say, "This nun is sensitive and touchy." With these words and others like them you try to hide the truth. Why not call things by their name? This sensitivity and touchiness is nothing more than a form of pride. Let's fight it wherever pride likes to hide, and make war on it without mercy. Of all the vices, of all the diseases of the soul, it's the most serious, the most damaging, especially because we are not ashamed of it as we are with the other vices, however less serious and less harmful to us they may be. The main reason that Jesus doesn't accomplish in us all that he would is because of this terrible obstacle of pride that not only prevents him from acting in us, but moves him away from us.

A Sermon for the Feast of Saint Stephen Harding

Our Rules, our Constitutions, our Usages teach us the particular kind of religious life that we must live and the special form of holiness for which we must strive. But it is especially in the school of those who have realized perfectly the ideal of our Order that we learn in a more vital way what makes up this characteristic holiness that must be ours. It is said that to take the pure water of a stream or river one must go back to the source. So to find the true spirit of an Order we must return to the founders, study their writings, their spirit, and especially, their example.[28]

Turned down for profession at Grottaferrata in June of 1919, through the help of Dom Norbert Mother Tecla entered Chimay, where she made her perpetual profession on September 8, 1921. During her novitiate at Grottaferrata she had benefited from the spiritual direction of Dom Norbert, who then continued to direct her at Chimay. In addition, at Chimay Mother Tecla profited from the teaching of Dom Anselm Le Bail and Dom Godefroid Belorgey,[29] who introduced her to the study of the Cistercian Fathers and Mothers, including Saint Lutgard, Saint Gertrude, and Beatrice of Nazareth. [30]

[Mother Pia's Formation]

We know that for Maria Gullini, who was to become Mother Pia, the encounter with Dom Norbert was decisive for her monastic vocation and that she made a retreat under his direction at the Trappist monastery of Grottaferrata in November 1916, which was followed by her entry into the French mon-

---

[28] Anthology of sermons given to the community of Grottaferrata, Archives of Scourmont.

[29] Dom Anselm Le Bail (1878–1956). Born in Brittany on December 31, 1878, he entered the Trappist monastery of Scourmont on May 21, 1904, and on October 4, 1913, was elected as the community's abbot, a position he held until his death in 1956. Godefroid Belorgey, monk of Scourmont Abbey, held various community positions: master of lay brothers, novice master, and prior. Named superior of Cîteaux in 1932, he was blessed as auxiliary abbot on September 14, 1933, a post he held until 1952. For a deeper understanding of the importance of the figure of Dom Anselm Le Bail for the renewal of the Cistercian Order of the Strict Observance, see Dom Armand Veilleux, "Un grand formateur monastique: Dom Anselme Le Bail," *Collectanea Cisterciensia* 63 (2001): 224–33.

[30] Pearse Aidan Cusack, "Abbess Thecla Fontana," *Hallel: A Review of Monastic Spirituality and Liturgy* 29, no. 2 (2004): 96–117.

astery of Laval on June 28, 1917. Dom Norbert continued to guide his spiritual daughter through correspondence and visits made to Laval on the occasion of the general chapter, which was held every year at Cîteaux. The annual retreat he directed in Laval in October 1921 was memorable. Even from the title of each conference we can realize the richness of his teaching at a time when preaching tended to be very moralistic.

Let us take a look at them in order to get a better idea: 1) The need to study Christ: to know, love, and live in intimacy with him, and to make him live in us, 2) The five dispositions that the knowledge of God will produce in us—admiration, adoration, respect, submission, and confidence, 3) The divinity of Jesus Christ, 4) The divine motherhood, 5) The mystery of Jesus Christ crucified, 6) The characteristics of Jesus the Savior, 7) Mary, co-redemptrix of humanity, 8) Jesus, the divine friend, 9) Jesus, the divine spouse, 10) The Eucharist, 11 and 12) Our incorporation into Christ, according to Saint Paul, 13) Our divine life is our sanctification, 14) Mortification, 15) The means to be used to work for our sanctification, 16) Mary's motherhood, 17) The humility of Jesus, 18) The love of Jesus, 19) Communion, 20) Conclusion: the life of prayer.[31] In her memories of Dom Norbert, Mother Pia wrote, "After this retreat we began to study the gospel with commentaries and synopses."[32]

---

[31] Archives of the Abbey of Scourmont.

[32] M. Pia Gullini, "Quelques souvenirs sur le Vénéré Père Dom Norbert," Grottaferrata 1931, Archives of Scourmont Abbey. It does not seem out of place to quote the entire passage: "It was a real success. One never heard him speak in this way. It had the effect of inflaming all souls for the better and to push them to an ever-deeper knowledge of Jesus, to love him even more. *We began to study the gospel* with commentaries and synopses. Some young religious, whose parents were well pleased to offer something, asked them for the eight-volume *Holy Scriptures* with commentary by Fillon, and other works of Fillon: *The Life of Jesus Christ* in three volumes. It was a real breath of supernatural life, the life of love lived by the ancient Cistercians, who so deeply loved the sacred books and whose spirituality is so simple: Jesus and nothing else besides him. But in such a relationship of intimacy, trust, abandonment!"

In this way Mother Pia was formed in a Christocentric spirituality ("Let us fall in love with the humanity of Christ, the man-God") that was Marian, eucharistic, and ecclesial. It was based on the Gospel, the Rule of Saint Benedict, the Cistercian fathers and mothers, and, in particular for Mother Pia, on Saint Lutgard and Saint Gertrude. One of her fellow religious recounts,

> Humility and obedience were her warhorses, and the indispensable substratum for everything was *love*.
> She detested envy and jealousy as among the worst obstacles to the flourishing of fraternal love and gave no truce to this enemy when she saw it in one or the other of her daughters.
> She had a lively sense of the majesty, the magnificence, the regality, and the greatness of God, before whom the only possible attitude was praise, adoration, thanksgiving, and abandonment. On one occasion she was in St. Peter's for a canonization, where she had a seat in the tribune among the very prim and proper. The assistants were seated, and the Sistine choir was singing a magnificent *Credo*. "All of a sudden," relates Mother Pia, "at the *descendit de coelis*, I had the lively sense of the majesty of God moving down towards us, and without realizing it I found that I had suddenly fallen on my knees."[33]

In 1931, the abbot of Scourmont asked Mother Pia to record her memories and the community's memories of Dom Norbert. This task also involved the transcription of his thoughts and advice to Mother Pia herself and to other nuns. Reading some of these tracts seems interesting and demonstrates how, through Dom Norbert's teaching, a certain parlance came into use in the community:

> A religious must be a spouse. Jesus has a great number of religious, but very few spouses, and he, the God-Man,

---

[33] Fara Crapanzano, Unpublished Memories, Archives of Vitorchiano.

needs to be loved from a heart that loves. A religious might be a woman, but if she doesn't have an ardent love for Jesus Christ her life is out of tune. In a contemplative order life without this great flame would be a vegetative life, an impossible life. Her life must be a life of love for him.

I leave these two principles: have a real respect for authority; the authority is Jesus. . . . Love your sisters for the love of Jesus. Become his, all for him. Jesus loves you. Love and believe, and never doubt, so as never to deserve that sad reproach that Jesus often addressed to the apostles: "men of little faith, why are you afraid?" He loves us because of his love. Let's give him the honor of having faith in him.

The religious woman belongs to Jesus. The troubles of the common life disappear for the religious who says to herself, "I am here for Jesus. Perhaps this small annoyance can be taken away? No? well then let's go forward." And this should not be a feeling, but a principle. You've got to have a bigger idea of Jesus, of his real presence in his house, because the monastery is his house.

Jesus is present in this house. A religious who does not think about him, but only about herself, is a horror!!

Holiness is not a luxury. We have to arrive there because it is the life of Jesus.

When you do something, say to him, "Do you like it?" and then, "Are you happy?" Don't we do this with the ones we love? We look at our beloved and say, "It's for you that I did this." And if Jesus responds, "Hey! Hey! There was a bit of self-love in that action," then we should answer, "Forgive me!"

Consider that Jesus always looks at you, and that he always takes care of you, and meanwhile, you forget about him! Jesus loves you dearly, but you do not render love for love. Therefore think about the seriousness of this!

Make small gifts for Jesus, but frequently. Don't be discouraged, make the first one, then another, and then a third, and so on until the evening. And before evening Jesus will receive many small gifts from you! But then just think of whether he will allow himself to be outdone in generosity!

He will give to his little bride grace upon grace and make her strong and generous. . . .[34]

A few months after Mother Pia's perpetual profession of July 16, 1922, the abbess of Laval[35] appointed Mother Pia as mistress of the lay sisters, who numbered about forty. We can see from the testimony of one of them how the young mistress engaged herself fully in the task of formation to which she had been assigned, and how in her teaching she echoed the words, thoughts, and concepts of Dom Norbert.

[One of the sisters at Laval comments:] I still remember some of her lessons to the lay sisters. One day, one of our sisters had been accused in a meeting of the community because she was not "regular" in observance. Mother Pia told her, "Sister, it seems as if you are in charge of all the chicken coops in France! Jesus has chosen you to be his bride, and you, because of self-will, act as a servant and relegate being a spouse to second place. Imagine a bride who takes good care of her husband, preparing his meals well and even his clothing, but never has time to be with him, to talk to him, and to live in intimacy with him! . . . Do you think he'd be happy? No, he needs affection and intimacy with her. Well then, Jesus expects this from you."

Another time she came to give a lesson with pictures of the Sacred Heart that she had made herself. Not all were done so well. Some were more beautiful than others, and she said, "Do you see these pictures, my sisters? All of you must be images of Jesus: it is our vow of conversion that asks us to become, day by day, a little more like Jesus. He is our model." And she devoted the whole lesson to explain this.

One day one of our sisters was accused of having woken up a sister who was snoring and prevented her from sleeping, but Mother Pia said, "Sister, but how could you dare to wake

---

[34] Gullini, "Quelques souvenirs."
[35] Lutgarde Hémery, Abbess of Laval from 1900 to 1944.

Jesus? Don't you know that everything you do to his sisters, you do to Jesus himself?" And she continued in this vein.[36]

[Mother Pia's Recollections of Sister Gabriella]

After this "intermission," in which we have tried, in a succinct manner, to give an idea of the environment that Sister Maria Gabriella encountered in Grotta, in the community, and the people directly involved in her formation, we go back to listen to Mother Pia speaking about her daughter from Dorgali:

> Her smile had become natural: she was always smiling. She was as affectionate as a child with the abbess and mistress, and she humbly marveled at their solicitude for her. She wanted no one to see her or look after her. The passion for being disregarded was something very important for her, walking a step at a time, without wishing to follow the more difficult roads, but allowing herself to be guided. . . .
>
> "She was averse to making herself known." She even eagerly wanted to be forgotten, left aside, and she did nothing to attract attention for the sake of making sure that we looked after her. One had to question her in order for her to talk about herself. This modesty sprang from her love: she wanted to be entirely for Jesus, to be his alone. She had to be entirely free for him; to do anything he wanted. She kept herself jealously for him. . . .
>
> . . . She had no demands: everything seemed free, unmerited, and priceless. She lived on gratitude. Her "thank you" was like the breath of her soul. . . .
>
> "Thank you . . . thank you . . . ." The gratitude in which she always lived expanded like an ocean into which her soul plunged and drowned. And she was never to leave it. On her lips, the words expressing this gratitude were

---

[36] Letter of Sr. M. L., Archives of Vitorchiano.

invariably simple and modest but had the quality of the depth that animated her. . . .

Love made her understand the necessity of this path of always going forward; it was that which constituted an aid to her strong will and her just and righteous reason, and gave her that quality of simplicity that one admired without even knowing why. *Bene omnia fecit* (*He did all things well*, Mark 7:37). But, since one should always act in this way, all of this was natural. She was the first to consider it natural. . . .[37]

When she entered the monastery, the terrain of her soul was already well cleared; she soaked up the instructions she received (mainly because she had a memory that helped her a lot), so much so that I marveled at her wisdom, which she learned from the experience of others. Her humble docility of spirit, common sense, and loyalty to grace led her in three and a half years of monastic life to the heights (of virtue). . . .

Only he—Only God—therefore "not I."

Nothing about me; otherwise, we would be two. . . .

Ecce . . . fiat mihi [*Behold, be it done unto me*, Luke 1:38]. Readiness and absence of personal self will.

Here also her consistency stands out: God, who knows everything and can do everything, brought her to surrender herself completely to him. . . .

Her docility, her abandonment came—it seems to me—because she intuited the greatness of God, and, without analyzing her feelings, she lived in the concrete adoration of the God who had chosen her and loved her. She felt so unworthy, so small, so nothing: this stemmed from her humility and gratitude. . . .

One cannot think of an interior life simpler than hers. No ascetic feats, nor did she make efforts to place herself in this or that degree of prayer: no baggage of devotions (supplementary prayers) or of practical additions to Mass and the Divine Office.

---

[37] Gullini, "Notebooks," p. 150 below.

> . . . She used to say the rosary and was very fond of the Stations of the Cross, which were placed in the corridor of the infirmary. . . .
> . . . she would not enter into a race for zeal or mystical flights for anything in the world. She was even reluctant to accept that such flights were to be desired. . . . she finished step by step, always without heroic appearances.
> The Lord himself in coming to meet her would set fire to the path that separated them. . . .
> . . . In all things she has her place among the great ascetic figures and mystical personages of her Order, the Order of Cîteaux, and the Trappists in particular. The monastery for her was simply Jesus, his love, his will, and his glory. She was his disciple and his bride, imitating the Blessed Virgin Mary, who welcomed Jesus in her womb, responding to the angel of the Annunciation: "*Ecce . . . fiat mihi.*"[38]

In some of the biographies of Sister Maria Gabriella we read the episode, narrated by Mother Pia herself, of the way, in a corner of the infirmary, she noted down the responses given by Sister Maria Gabriella for some of the mothers and novices. We read in Mother Pia's Notebooks to Gaston Zananiri:

> Sr. M. Gabriella knew how to find for each person a word "ad hoc" so that one could say it was inspired! It was especially so when I heard what she said to a novice who was very stubborn in her "good" ideas: "For me, when the superiors say something, *it would be impossible for me to think differently.*" . . . Notice the word *think* and consider it in the context of her very strong personality, her former stubbornness, and her fastidiousness.[39]

---

[38] Gullini, "Notebooks."

[39] In a letter to Rev. Fr. Cappio from Fille-Dieu, Mother Pia says about this sentence, "neither Dore nor Zananiri has cited the letter, in order not to shock those delicate spirits. But for me it was revealing of her holiness, and outstanding holiness. As I knew the personality of this daughter, this renunciation of her judgment, a result of her will and effort, she was capable of a

And Mother Tecla, for her part, speaking of Gabriella's docility in response to Father Meloni's decision to send her to the Trappist monastery of Grottaferrata, comments,

> He was the one who directed her here. Full confidence in the sacred minister guided the young girl Maria Sagheddu in her choice [of where to enter]. This total submission of intellect and will remained the hallmark of her spirituality. . . . She venerated obedience. . . . In one of her meetings with me, with her usual calm she stated, "I have no other program other than to give up my will," and with that, Sr. Gabriella renounced even her judgment. This, in my opinion, is the shortcut to reach sanctity. So it's no wonder that Sr. Gabriella progressed so much in a short time.[40]

Like Gaston Zananiri, it is normal for us today to wonder about the deep motive that might lead a person to offer her very life for a cause dear to the heart of Christ. Mother Pia answers thus:

> You ask me if the holocaust of one's very life is a Cistercian tradition. I believe it is a need for every generous soul, especially those in the cloister. We have nothing else but ourselves; we have given everything. By our vows we gave ourselves in the normal way; now we would like to place a greater emphasis on the offering, adding to it a meaning of suffering, consummation, and the renunciation of life, with the acceptance of a premature death.

---

heroic degree of many virtues and primarily of *faith*" (M. M. Pia Gullini, Romont, Feb. 12, 1958, Archives of Vitorchiano).

[40] M. Tecla Fontana, "Memoirs" [*Mie memorie della cara consorella Sr. Maria Gabriella, che lasciò questa terra d'esilio il 23 aprile 1939*], 1951 manuscript, Archives of Vitorchiano. Continuing her memoirs, at one point Mother Tecla says, "Within a few months her disposition was continually improving; some time ago she said that her personal program was the renunciation of her will, and shortly before her profession, she was saying, 'I'm not looking for anything other than the glory of God.'"

Maria Gabriella walked along, at her own pace, calm and safe, to eternal happiness. But the pain was unbearable at times, and she could not hold back the tears. The Rev. Mother noticed it:

> "You cried, little one? Why?"
> "Because don't I know how to suffer well. I don't feel the joy of suffering. I want to dominate my suffering with the spirit, and I do not know how to accept it."
> And her good sense finally came to the conclusion: "But . . . if we rejoice . . . we don't suffer any more."[41]

It is always touching to read this page of the biography of Mother Dore, as "the wedding day" of Mother Pia's daughter was approaching:

> In the evening, with a calm smile and beaming, she pronounced her usual short phrase, welcoming Rev. Mother saying, "How good the Lord is!" with an accent that was always new. At the same time, with bright eyes and an uplifted face, she slightly raised her arms. Rev. Mother, who had penetrated her soul, especially after the great trial of the hospital, bent over this flower with devotion, respect, and holy fear, and, enclosed in supernatural affection, mother and daughter understood one another.
> "I come to prepare you for the nuptials." That was the abbess's greeting upon entering. She spoke about divine love, and the flower opened up in that intimacy with a lovely scent. Remaining like this for a long time, Sr. Gabriella was enraptured in God, who was so good to her, and Rev. Mother was moved at such supernatural splendor.[42]

---

[41] *Marie Gabrielle: Une vie offerte pour l'unité chrétienne, par une religieuse de la Trappe* (Brussels: Sécretariat de l'Unité Chrétienne, 1956), 27.
[42] Maria Giovanna Dore, *Dalla Trappa per l'Unità della Chiesa: Suor Maria Gabriella (1914–1939)* (Brescia: Morcelliana, 1946), 141.

Mother and daughter, their two lives joined in a single offering, in a single undivided love for the "gentle Lord" of their lives, were both consumed, although differently, for his glory and so that all the children of the one Father might be ONE, now and always.

Sister Maria Paola Santachiara, OCSO
Vitorchiano, April 29, 2009
50th anniversary of the death of Mother Maria Pia Gullini

Doing Nothing, Achieving All: Blessed Maria Gabriella of Unity

Sister Maria Gabriella knew she would be dead within a year's time. With her abbess's permission she left her room in the infirmary and went to the novitiate. There she gathered and destroyed all her writings. "Sparisco io, sparisca tutto," she said: "If I'm going, it all goes." Twenty-four years old, Maria Gabriella wanted to die as she had lived, silent and unnoticed. People who knew her in her childhood would remember nothing exceptional about Maria Gabriella Sagheddu. Her sisters in the monastery would recall nothing particularly outstanding. This was her desire: to be a saint without attracting attention.

Sister Maria Gabriella died in the spring of 1939. She had been in the monastery of Grottaferrata barely three years. By 1940, her first biography was published. Soon several editions in several languages appeared. Other biographies followed, and Maria Gabriella's renown spread. Sister Maria Gabriella's tomb in the crypt of her undistinguished Trappistine monastery in the Colli Albani outside Rome became the destination of a stream of pilgrims and devotees from Europe, Great Britain, and North America. In 1958 the process for the canonization of Maria Gabriella Sagheddu was opened. Finally, in 1995, people reading Pope John Paul II's Encyclical Letter on the commitment to ecumenism, *Ut unum sint*, found Maria Gabriella Sagheddu, native of Dorgali, Sardegna, and nun of Grottaferrata, offered to them as the model for carrying out every Christian's duty to pray for Christian unity.

Sister Maria Gabriella did not succeed in disappearing. Nor did she entirely destroy all her writings. There remained some reading notes and a collection of forty letters, mostly to her mother and to her abbess. The letters taken together are a story of a soul, honest and convincing, like the bread of Maria Gabriella's native Dorgali. Given her age and provenance, they are also puzzling. The reader is struck as a relative in Dorgali was: her letters seem to be written by someone else. "They are on a level superior to Maria Gabriella's ability, who had no more than a sixth-grade education." It is impossible to find in these documents anything that would explain her efforts to "destroy her writings." A constant of Maria Gabriella Sagheddu's personality, from childhood to deathbed, was her limpid honesty. The content of her letters is discreet, the style parsimonious, yet there is never a doubt that all the truth is there, as Maria Gabriella wished it to be told. The letters provide no way of knowing what she was trying to keep hidden. And this is precisely the clue to the matter.

For Sister Maria Gabriella did have a secret. It was the one thing she never wrote home about. Her secret was a decision she had made. Once she had made her decision with the approval of her superiors, she never mentioned it again, not once, not even to them. Besides Maria Gabriella's two or three superiors, only her mother, Caterina Sagheddu, and Dom Benedict Ley of the Anglican Benedictine Abbey of Nashdom would be privy to her secret before her death. The best guess, then, as to what Maria Gabriella wished to destroy with her writings was this unique decision, her only secret.

As it happened, she was right. For her secret, made public after her death, resulted in the very thing she had tried to preclude, attention drawn to herself. Maria Gabriella, in January 1938, had decided to offer her life for the cause of Christian Unity. Her secret was the soul of her life, the key to her death, the form of her sanctity. It also proved to forge the destiny of her monastic community. Six months after her offering, Maria Gabriella's abbess, Madre Pia Gullini, wrote to Sister Maria Gabriella's mother. Madre Pia told Caterina Sagheddu of her daughter's offering. She went on to say that her daughter was gravely ill with tuberculosis. Maria Gabriella died on April 23, 1939. On April 26, Madre Pia again wrote to Caterina. It was a long letter, woman to woman—better, mother to mother. In minute detail Madre Pia described to Mamma Caterina her daughter's final hours:

> From Thursday the twentieth . . . the afternoon of that Saturday . . . At four o'clock . . . At half past five, very tranquilly, she ceased to breathe. She lowered her eyelids—as when she was unable to speak, to say, "Yes." Then she raised her eyelids again. She was already with her Lord, whom she loved so much that she offered the sacrifice of her young life for the union of the separated churches. It was Good Shepherd Sunday, and the gospel spoke thus: "I have other sheep, which are not of this fold; I must bring them also."[1]

The next morning, Madre Pia spoke to the assembled nuns of Grottaferrata: "Sister Maria Gabriella was a real Trappistine . . . . She forgot herself completely in her quest for the glory of God. . . . She passed smilingly among us without ever attracting attention to herself, without ever causing anyone to complain about her . . . except for the anguish they felt when they learned she was ill and discovered the hidden treasure they possessed."

Sister Maria Gabriella was Madre Pia's *figliola*, her little daughter. Maria Gabriella thought of herself as a "pygmy in the way of the spirit"; to Pia, she was "wisdom's own wisdom." Later, Madre Pia would say that Sister Maria Gabriella was a "pacifying light." But if Maria Gabriella Sagheddu was light, Pia Gullini was the lens focusing it, and Grottaferrata the textured surface upon which it fell to be seen. Maria Elena Gullini was, by her own account, a woman of strong and fiery

---

[1] M. Pia Gullini, "Autograph Notebooks of M. Pia Gullini: Responses to Gaston Zananiri's Questions," Vitorchiano Archives, 1953; pp. 134–35 above.

temperament who had let herself fall in love with the incarnate God. She entered the Order of Cistercians of the Strict Observance at Laval, France, in 1916, at the age of twenty-one. She was given the name Pia after Pope Pius X, from whom she had received her First Communion.

After ten years of Trappist life at Laval, Sister Pia was sent to the monastery at Grottaferrata in her native Italy. "Grotta," as it was called, was a fervent, culturally backward, materially poor Trappistine community. When Pia arrived at Grotta she brought with her from Laval a monastic culture and spiritual vigor grounded in liturgy and doctrine. Elected abbess in 1931, four years before Maria Gabriella entered, Madre Pia opened to her daughters the ascetic doctrines of J. P. de Caussade, Francis de Sales, Thérèse of Lisieux, and Dom Vital Lehodey.

Above all, Madre Pia thrust this willing but unsuspecting community into an apostolate practically unheard of for Italian women religious of the time, let alone Trappistines of any nationality: the newly opened "ecumenical movement." Madre Pia had been introduced in the mid-'30s to the hopes and challenges of ecumenism by a French laywoman she had befriended while still at Laval. By 1936 she was in regular contact with Abbé Paul Courturier, the great promoter of the Week of Prayer for Christian Unity. Through Abbé Couturier, Pia began an active exchange of letters with the Anglican Benedictine Dom Benedict Ley. Madre Pia's idea for the 1940 biography of Maria Gabriella was a farsighted tactic in the service of Christian Unity.

In the 1950s Pia would remark, "I am in close contact with the Brothers of Taizé, whose young founder[2] together with his mother and brother Max came to Grotta in 1950. They all descended to the tomb of Sister M. Gabriella." The friendship between Madre Pia and Madame Schutz lasted until the latter's death. In 1983, Br. Roger would be in the Basilica of St. Paul Outside the Walls when Pope John Paul II beatified Sister Maria

---

[2] Roger Schutz.

Gabriella, Patroness of Unity. In 1947, the Anglican Benedictine Dom Benedict Ley paid his first visit to Grottaferrata. Lodged in the chaplain's quarters at Grotta, Dom Benedict took every opportunity to spend time in prayer at the tomb of Sister Maria Gabriella. With Grotta as home base, he met with Monsignor Montini of the Vatican Secretariat of State to discuss Anglican-Catholic relations in England. Within the next decade Dom Benedict would visit Grotta two more times. As a result of Dom Benedict's reports, some fifty Anglicans, Orthodox, and Protestants from England visited Grotta from 1948 to 1951 alone. All were deeply impressed by the warm and sisterly welcome they received from Madre Pia and the other nuns. "I cannot tell you how good the Trappistines of Grottaferrata have been to me," reported one Anglican visitor in 1949. "They gave a magnificent dinner in honor of my mission, a true *agape*, and even gave me presents!"

In their news bulletin for 1950 the nuns of Grotta announced to the Cistercian Order, "Visitors to Grotta have been almost continuous during this Holy Year, coming from the many parts of Italy as well as from outside. Among our pilgrim friends are a good number of separated brethren. . . . In September an important international meeting of specialists in the area of Christian Unity was held at the Greek Catholic Abbey of St. Nilus in Grottaferrata. Given our proximity to St. Nilus and the interest the topic has for us, we were able closely to follow the three days of conferences." Madre Pia Gullini's ardor for Christian Unity would find its match in Sister Maria Gabriella Sagheddu's secret appropriation of the prayer of Jesus, "that all may be one." If for Pia ecumenism was a sign of the times eliciting her prophetic ecclesial response, for Maria Gabriella it was the longing of her Bridegroom: "Jesus, I love you! I thank you! In these few words all is said; . . . may you be glorified in me."

The notoriety that accrued to the Trappistines of Grottaferrata from their abbess's zeal for ecumenism and the overwhelming success of the 1940 biography of Maria Gabriella did not go unnoticed by the authorities of the Cistercian Order.

They watched it with no small degree of incomprehension. The outcome for Pia was the swift, premature abandonment of her abbatial charge in 1951, and immediate exile to Switzerland. By that time, Grotta had been immersed in ecumenism for over a decade. To say the community of Trappistines was ahead of its time is to say too little. On the one hand, this group of truly humble, poor, hardworking nuns was the perfect fulfillment of the wish Pius XI made before the consistory of March 24, 1924. The pontiff had said, "We will be obliged to all Catholics who strive, under the impulse of divine grace, to facilitate admittance to the true faith for their separated brothers, whoever these may be, by dispelling their prejudices, keeping in view unadulterated Catholic teaching, and especially making evident in themselves the features of disciples of Christ, for there is love."

On the other hand, an historian of the times says that in 1930s Italy, "the dispute between Catholics and Protestants was . . . mean-spirited to the point of lacking any civility. Catholics and Protestants regarded each other with hostility, as adversaries, full of suspicion and anger. . . ." While some Church authorities seemed bent on defending the bases of disunion, Madre Pia and the community of Grotta were among the most fervent and active supporters in Italy of the Week of Prayer for Christian Unity. If Rome understood reunion in terms of returning to the fold by the renunciation of errors, Madre Pia followed the line of Paul Courturier: to pray that the will of Jesus be done by the means he chooses. "It is from [the] stance of friendship," she said, "that Catholics and Protestants need to start in order to find—like brothers—the common ground. . . . It is love that matters, love that is union, reciprocity."

There is little doubt that the young Sardinian, Sister Maria Gabriella Sagheddu, was the hidden and silent center of Madre Pia's bold and courageous service to Grotta and to the Church. "I go to see her every evening," Pia confided before Maria Gabriella died, "and I confess to you that for me this is a joy, a strength, true spiritual refreshment." In 1948, Madre Pia wrote a letter to a woman doing research for a new biography of Maria Gabriella: "Years of experience with this question of 'Reunion' . . . have led me to understand that the success of your book will rest on the fact that there is nothing whatsoever about her life that anyone could use as a fulcrum for controversy. . . . Those who are ignorant of the problem will come to understand it from the example of Sister Maria Gabriella. Those who are experts will find in her a repose they had never known before, a pacifying light, a new horizon disposing them to love rather than debate."

On Sunday, January 16, 1938, the fifty nuns of the Trappistine community of Grottaferrata outside Rome were gathered in the chapter room of the monastery to listen to the teaching of their abbess, Mother Pia Gullini. Among them was twenty-three-year-old Sister Maria Gabriella Sagheddu. This particular Sunday, Mother Pia read aloud and commented upon the tract by Abbé Paul Couturier announcing the 1938 "Unity Week," today known as the "Week of Prayer for Christian Unity." The "Unity Week" was the annual crusade of prayer from the eighteenth to the twenty-fifth of January for the healing of divisions and the reunion of the church.

In 1932, the French priest Paul Couturier had begun actively to promote Unity Week, lending to it his idea of "spiritual ecumenism." He understood that external material unity had to be preceded by an essential inner unity, expressed by a great number of souls praying and offering themselves in union with the offering of Jesus. He liked to envision an "invisible monastery," a community of prayer and sacrifice that was not limited by denomination or state in life. In 1936 Abbé Couturier published his first tract. The following year, 1937, he sent out more than 1500 copies of his tract. For the first time, at the request of Madre Pia, a copy of his tract arrived at Grottaferrata and was read by her in chapter to the nuns.

Now, on January 16, 1938, Mother Pia for the second time read Abbé Couturier's annual tract to her Trappistine sisters.

> Prayer will remain the living and luminous center [of the work for Christian unity].... Openly and simultaneously participated in by all throughout the fractured Church during these days of the 18th to the 25th of January, prayer will lead the Church along the way of Unity. The suffering of disunity alone can open the hearts of all Christians and make them listen to the sorrow hidden in the prayer of Christ to his Father at the Last Supper . . . "may they be one in us . . . that the world may believe."

The tract continued: "May there be a harvest of many offerings to the Spirit from obscure and hidden lives," Mother Pia read, "to collaborate in his great work of reunion of Christians."

The Trappistines of Grottaferrata listened as Abbé Couturier went on to give three examples of Christians who had recently offered their lives for the cause of Christian unity. Among them he named— a revelation to many of the nuns—Grottaferrata's own Madre dell'Immaculata Scalvini. Seventy-eight years old, Madre dell'Immaculata had the previous January offered her life for the cause of Christian unity in response to Abbé Paul's tract read in chapter. She died a month later.

Listening to these appeals to spiritual ecumenism, Sister Maria Gabriella could not help being moved. She had once said to her novice director, "I would not know how to keep account of my interior life. I simply look for occasions to make sacrifices. . . . I look them in the face and act." It is no surprise, then, that soon after hearing Abbé Couturier's 1938 tract, Sister Maria Gabriella Sagheddu knocked at the Madre Pia's door and entered the abbess's office. "Let me offer my life," Madre Pia recalled her asking. "What is it worth anyway? I am doing nothing. I have never done anything. You yourself said that one might make this offering with permission." After prudent discernment, permission was granted the young Trappistine to "offer her life" for the cause of Christian Unity.

It is difficult to write about Maria Gabriella Sagheddu. It is difficult because her life is not a matter of all those dramatic patterns that most of us in the Western world think of as "real life"—events, talents and accomplishments, successes and failures. Nor is it a matter of relationships, at least not the kinds of relationships that Western Europeans and North Americans entering the third millennium are exposed to in sitcoms, entertainment weeklies, and radio talk shows. Rather, Maria Gabriella's life, at least after her conversion at eighteen, was quintessentially spiritual. "My only desire," she once said, "is to . . . make myself a saint." This was self love, but not selfishness and egoism. She wanted to be a saint, not for her sake but for God's and her neighbors'. Someone said of her, "she was not spoiled," and hardly more need be said. As a young adult and as a nun her life was a shot arrow splitting the air, not so much propelled as drawn with ever-increasing velocity by and to the target.

Maria Gabriella Sagheddu entered the Trappistines of Grottaferrata on Monday, September 30, 1935. She was twenty-one. One of her neighbors in Dorgali said later, "When I heard Maria Sagheddu was planning on becoming a nun I couldn't believe it. . . . She didn't seem to me to be the type called to the convent." Many others would have agreed. Two contradictory sets of traits marked Maria Sagheddu as a child. On the one hand, she was honest, bright, and optimistic. Although she had to quit school at twelve years of age, she was an excellent student. She loved to read, especially novels, and was always ready to help other students with their work. Duty, loyalty, and obedience were primary values for the young Maria. Physically strong and healthy, she did not hesitate to bear the heavier parts of domestic or field work.

But at the same time, young Maria was mischievous, impatient, and demanding. She always wanted to be right, to have the last word. She expected others to be as honest and forthright as she herself. "Go to hell" and "Damn" (*Va alla malora! Accidenti!*) she would say when people didn't live up to her expectations. If something didn't go her way, she stamped her feet in anger and frustration.

Both of these sets of traits, increasingly transformed, set in order, and put at the service of a single-minded goal, would color Maria Gabriella's character for the rest of her life. In her childhood and early adolescence, Maria's religious practice was minimal. This did not pass unnoticed in the traditional Catholic culture of Dorgali, largely centered on the parish and religious devotions. Baptized a week after her birth, Maria made her first communion at the age of ten, but after that, except for the Sunday obligation, neglected the sacraments and attendance at church services. "She wasn't much given to church," people remembered. She preferred reading novels and playing cards and board games. If her mother urged her to go to evening Benediction, Maria might respond, "Go yourself!" or, "There's no obligation. Leave me alone," and remain intent on her book or her game.

But at the age of eighteen, a quiet revolution took place in the soul of Maria. She never talked about it. She did not have to. The revolution bore the fruits of conversion, and they spoke for her. She joined Catholic Action and began giving religious instruction to children. She regularly visited the sick, taking particular interest in a young woman with an illegitimate son. She established a friendship with a girl who had a poor reputation and helped her overcome her destructive behavior. She never refused people asking for a handout, and she would often rise early in the morning to help neighbors with the bread making. It was recalled that "she began to meditate and to make the monthly adoration. . . . She went to confession almost every week and received daily communion. . . . I often saw her kneeling in prayer before the Blessed Sacrament. What struck me was her attitude of deep recollection. There was nothing sugary about it; rather, there was a great austerity." Not long after her conversion, Maria Gabriella looked into a religious vocation. She had seen other young women leave Dorgali to enter Grottaferrata. Now she spoke to her pastor, Don Basilio Meloni, about the possibility for herself. "You want to go to Grottaferrata, then?" Don Meloni asked her. "Send me where you will," Maria replied. "Then to Grottaferrata you will go," decided Don Meloni.

In July of 1938, seven months after Sister Maria Gabriella's oblation, Mother Pia wrote a long letter to the Anglican Benedictine Dom Benedict Ley. Dom Benedict, novice master of Nashdom Abbey, England, had for some time already been an "ecumenical" friend of Mother Pia's. Mother Pia told Dom Benedict,

> As I did last year, I had read in chapter the invitation of our friend Don Couturier. A young professed nun, just twenty-four years old, asked to make the same offering as Madre dell'Immacolata. I gave her permission. . . . Now Sister is in the infirmary with tuberculosis, she who was one of the strongest in the community, with absolutely no family history of this illness. . . . It is Sr. Maria Gabriella, a beautiful daughter . . . gifted with uncommon intelligence. Only now that the Lord is calling do I realize what a treasure she is.

A month earlier, Mother Pia had written to Sister Maria Gabriella's mother Caterina Sagheddu, informing her of her daughter's grave condition: "For me, it is a great sorrow. But knowing that Sister Maria Gabriella offered herself to the Lord for one of the most noble causes, the hasty union of the dissident churches, I realize that the Lord has accepted the offering. Your daughter told me this: 'From that day when I offered myself, I have not been well.'" Over a period of forty days in a Roman sanitarium, Sister Maria Gabriella underwent humiliating treatment that only aggravated her tubercular condition. She returned to Grottaferrata in May 1938. On April 23, 1939, just after her twenty-fifth birthday, Sister Maria Gabriella died in the arms of Madre Pia in the monastery infirmary. In her final agony Mother Pia asked Maria Gabriella, "You offer it all for Unity, don't you?" The dying nun replied, simply, "Yes."

Madre Pia wrote to Maria Gabriella's mother Caterina informing her of her daughter's death. She recalled that April 23 was Good Shepherd Sunday that year: "The gospel spoke of the other sheep that are not of this fold that I must bring also." Mother Pia reminded Caterina Sagheddu that her daughter "loved her Lord so much as to offer him the sacrifice of her young life for the union of the separated Churches." When Anglican Benedictine Dom Benedict Ley got word of Maria Gabriella's death, he pointed out that April 23 was also the Feast of St. George, Patron of England. "She will take our . . . efforts . . . for Unity under her special protection," he said. Dom Benedict was kind enough to send condolences to Caterina Sagheddu: "I hope you will allow me to tell you," he wrote, "that the sacrifice of your daughter compels me to a greater fidelity to Christ and to a more intimate prayer for the reunion of all Christians under the Pope."

Except for such brief remarks as those quoted above to her abbess, Sister Maria Gabriella made no explicit reference to her "offering" for unity. Nevertheless, the collection of forty letters written by Maria Gabriella that survive reveals that her offering was the core of her identity as a Christian and as a Cistercian nun. Her offering of her life for unity gave specific form to her spirituality. It became the place for her encounter with God.

Sister Maria Gabriella's letters are like the best of letters, spontaneous, intimate, at times random and always self-revealing and engaging. In them Maria Gabriella uses three sets of images, or three languages, to write about her offering. The language of "holy abandonment" is reminiscent of J. P. de Caussade and Thérèse of Lisieux. Spousal or nuptial imagery recalls Bernard of Clairvaux, Jan van Ruysbroeck, and John of the Cross. And the semantic fields of love, joy, glory, consecration, and fullness are clear echoes of the last discourse of Jesus, his prayer for unity, in the Gospel of John, chapters 13 through 17, chapters that Maria Gabriella read with particular intensity during her final illness. She can so easily blend these traditional languages that it is evident that she made each of them her own.

In the examples that follow, the italic print isolates the language of abandonment, the nuptial imagery, and the echoes of John's gospel. In a letter from July of 1938 to her former spiritual director in Dorgali, Maria Gabriella assures him, "*I will be happy and my happiness is truly great.* What *joy* to be able to suffer something for the love of Jesus and for souls. I have made a great act of *abandonment* into the hands of the Lord, and my heart and my soul are now immersed in a profound *peace, a great joy.* When I think of the blessed day [when] *I will go above to embrace the Celestial Spouse,* then my *joy and my happiness surpass anything on earth*!" In April of 1938 Sister Maria Gabriella wrote her mother from the sanitarium, "Pray for me, that I will always *glorify the Lord in doing his divine will* in whatever form it takes. . . . I have *offered myself* entirely to my Jesus and *do not take back my word.*" A few weeks later, after a sputum analysis had proven positive, she wrote to Madre Pia,

> The first day I suffered a great deal; then, yesterday afternoon, I felt a great force take root in my heart, and I *resigned myself* fully to *the will of God,* accepting to suffer *for his glory* . . . . I assure you that *my sacrifice is total,* because from dawn to night I do nothing but *renounce my will,* my hopes, my desires, and everything that is in me, whether holy or defective, in everything and for everything. At first there was no way to bend my heart; now I truly understand that *the glory of God* and being a victim does not consist in doing great things but in *the total sacrifice* of one's own "I."

Again, writing to her mother: "The people of *the world* say we are selfish, closing ourselves up in a convent and thinking only of ourselves. That's not true. We live a life of *continual sacrifice* to the point of *immolation for the salvation of souls.* . . . In the monastery, every act, even the most repugnant, even doing nothing at all, when it is commanded by *obedience,* brings with it great merit." In another letter, to Don Meloni, Sister Maria Gabriella confided,

> Living in *abandonment,* I have not had to regret the past even once; what's more, I am even certain about what the future will be and sure that Jesus will do what is for his *greater glory* and what is best for my sanctification. . . .

Jesus has *chosen* me as a privileged one of his love, giving me suffering to make me more *like him*, and for that I am *perfectly happy*, and I thank him. I think I will never arrive at understanding enough *the love Jesus shows me* in offering me this cross."

It was the Church's ascetical tradition that gave Sister Maria Gabriella Sagheddu a language for expressing her deepest hopes and most intimate experiences of God. But her hopes and experiences themselves cannot be reduced to repetitions of classical formulas, nor dismissed as merely derived. If Maria Gabriella's response of faith is to be accurately located in the history of Christian spirituality, it would have to be in a Benedictine monasticism grounded in *lectio divina* and the liturgy. Pope John Paul II affirmed this in his homily on the occasion of the beatification of Maria Gabriella, January 25, 1983. She had the capacity, the pope said, "to receive and put into practice with 'the intelligence of love' St. Benedict's 'school of the Lord's service.' . . . It was precisely in her fidelity to listening that the young Maria Sagheddu succeeded in realizing that 'conversion of heart' that St. Benedict asks of his children; conversion of heart that is the true and primary source of unity." Maria Gabriella's life of conversion and the gift of herself to God in response to God's inviting love are original examples of biblical faith. They are as original and as uniquely her own as the *fiat* of Mary of Nazareth, as Jesus' "I have come . . . to give my life as a ransom for all," and as Saint Paul's "In my flesh I complete what is lacking in Christ's afflictions for the sake of his body, that is, the church."

Maria Gabriella made this act of faith while still in Dorgali: "Just let God call me, and I am ready." On the day of her monastic profession she renewed it: "In the simplicity of my heart, O Lord, I gladly offer you everything. You have been pleased to call me to yourself and . . . I have given everything that was in my power to give." Finally, some months before her death Maria Gabriella confessed, "I have abandoned myself totally into the hands of the Lord. . . . I feel I love my Spouse with all my heart, but I want to love him even more. I want to love him for those who do not love him, for those who despise him, for those who offend him: in short, my desire is nothing but to love."

"Blessed Maria Gabriella Sagheddu," said John Paul II in his beatification homily, "became a sign of the times and a model of that 'Spiritual Ecumenism' of which the Second Vatican Council reminded us. She encourages us to look with optimism—over and above the inevitable difficulties that are ours as human beings—to the marvelous prospects of ecclesial unity, whose progressive verification is linked with the ever deeper desire to be converted to Christ, in order to make active and effective his yearning: *Ut omnes unum sint!*"

Mark Scott, OCSO
New Melleray Abbey, Iowa

Bibliography

Acta Sanctae Sedis 27 (1894–1895): 65.

Bartoli, Maristella. "La beata M. Gabriella Sagheddu." Unpublished conferences 2003–2004, Scuola Cultura Monastica del monastero S. Benedetto delle benedettine dell'Adorazione Perpetua, Milan.

———. *A Life for Unity: Sr. Maria Gabriella*. Trans. Sr. Maria Jeremiah. New York: New City Press, 1990.

Benedict. *Saint Benedict's Rule for Monasteries*. Trans. Leonard Doyle. Collegeville, MN: Liturgical Press, 1948.

Bottasso, Teresa. "Diary of Mother Terese Bottasso." Unpublished.

Boyer, Charles. "L'idea di Paul Wattson." *Unitas* (1956): 161–65.

———. *Unità cristiana e movimento ecumenico*. Rome: Universale Studium, 1955.

Cabiddu, Gonario. *Lettere di una figlia scappata di casa*. Sassari: Stamperia artistica, 1982.

Cabizzosu, Tonino. *Maria Michela Dui, una trappista barbaricina vittima per i sacerdoti*. Cagliari: Grafiche Ghiani, 2005.

———. "Una vita spesa per la santificazione del clero." *L'Osservatore Romano*, 2 March 2005.

Caneva, Anna Maria. *Il riformatore della Trappa: Vita di Armand Jean De Rancé*. Rome: Città Nuova, 1996.

Cantimpré, Thomas. *Vita Lutgardis*. In *Thomas of Cantimpré: The Collected Saints' Lives: Abbot John of Cantimpré, Christina the Astonishing, Margaret of Ypres, and Lutgard of Aywières*. Ed. Barbara Newman. Trans. Margot H. King and Barbara Newman. Medieval Women, vol. 19. Turnhout, Belgium: Brepols, 2008.

Carpinello, Mariella. *Il monachesimo femminile*. Milan: Mondadori, 2002.

Crapanzano, Fara. "Unpublished Memories." Archives of Vitorchiano.

Cusack, Pearse Aidan. "Abbess Thecla Fontana." *Hallel: A Review of Monastic Spirituality and Liturgy* 29, no. 2 (2004): 96–117.

———. *Blessed Gabriella of Unity: A Patron for the Ecumenical Movement*. Ros Cré, Ireland: Cistercian Press, 1995.

Della Volpe, Monica. *La strada della gratitudine: Suor Maria Gabriella*. Milan: Jaca Books, 1983.

———. "A Model and a Guide along the Path of Ecumenism." *L'Osservatore Romano*, 17 January 2001.

Dore, Maria Giovanna. *Amore e sacrificio per l'Unità della Chiesa. Suor Maria Gabriella della Trappa di Grottaferrata*. Rome: Pia Società S. Paolo, 1940.

———. *Dalla Trappa per l'Unità della Chiesa: Suor Maria Gabriella (1914–1939)*. Foreword by Igino Giordani. Brescia: Morcelliana, 1940.

———. *Suor Maria Gabriella della Trappa di Grottaferrata: Amore e sacrificio per l'unità cristiana*. Rome: Edizioni Paoline, 1940.

Driscoll, Martha. *A Silent Herald of Unity: The Life of Maria Gabriella Sagheddu*. Cistercian Studies Series 199. Kalamazoo, MI: Cistercian Publications, 1990.

Fontana, Tecla. "Memoirs" [= *Mie memorie della cara consorella Sr. Maria Gabriella, che lasciò questa terra d'esilio il 23 aprile 1939*, 1951]. Vitorchiano Abbey Archives. Manuscript, Archives of Vitorchiano.

Francis, Pope. *Gaudete et exsultate*: Apostolic Exhortation on the Call to Holiness in Today's World. http://w2.vatican.va/content/francesco/en/apost_exhortations/documents/papa-francesco_esortazione-ap_20180319_gaudete-et-exsultate.html.

Fronteddu, Gabriele. "La Beata Maria Gabriella: Da social di Azione Cattolica a Beata per l'Unità dei cristiani." *Convegno Diocesano*, Dorgali, April 23, 2006.

Gannon, David. *Father Paul of Graymoor*. New York: The Macmillan Company, 1951.

Gullini, M. Pia. "Appunti della Rev. Madre su Suor Maria Gabriella / Notes of Mother Pia." Vitorchiano Archives.

———. *Lettere e scritti di Madre Pia*. Ed. Ennio Francia. Rome: Messa degli artisti, 1971.

———. "Notebooks of Mother Pia." Vitorchiano Archives.

———. "Quelques souvenirs sur le Vénéré Père Dom Norbert." Grottaferrata 1931, Archives of Scourmont Abbey.

Ildegarda di Bingen. *Ordo virtutum: Il cammino di Anima verso la salvezza*. Ed. Maria Tabaglio. San Pietro in Cariano: Il Segno di Gabrielli, 1999.

John Paul II, Pope. *Ut Unum Sint*. http://w2.vatican.va/content /john-paul-ii/en/encyclicals/documents/hf_jp-ii_enc_2505 1995_ut-unum-sint.html.

Leclercq, Jean. "Blessed Maria Gabriella Sagheddu: In Praise of Ordinariness." *Cistercian Studies Quarterly* 18, no. 3 (1983): 231–39.

Maccalli, Mario. *Madre dell'Immacolata*. Crema, Italy: Artigrafiche Leva, 1984.

Marie Gabrielle: Une vie offerte pour l'unité chrétienne, par une religieuse de la Trappe. Brussels: Sécretariat de l'Unité Chrétienne, 1956.

Merton, Thomas: *What Are These Wounds? The Life of a Cistercian Mystic, St. Lutgarde of Aywières*. Milwaukee: Bruce Publishing Company, 1950.

Miquel, Pierre. "Monachisme et oecuménisme." *Lettre de Ligugé* 219, no. 3 (1983): 1.

Morganti, M. Marta. *Maria Giovanna Dore*. Brescia: Morcelliana, 2001.

Penco, Gregorio. *Il monachesimo frà spiritualità e cultura*. Milan: Mondadori, 2000.

Piccardo, Cristiana. *Alla scuola della libertà: Riflessioni sulla vita monastica*. Milan: Ancora, 1992.

———. *Pedagogia Viva*. Milan: Jaca Books, 1999.

Piovano, Aldaberto, and Maria Ignazia Angelini. "Il monachesimo come luogo di incontro ecumenico." *Ora et Labora* 58, nos. 1 and 2 (2003).

Positio super virtutibus: Beatificationis et Canonizationis Mariae Gabriellae Sagheddu, moniale professae O.C.S.O.

Quattrocchi, Paolino Beltrame. *La Beata Maria Gabriella dell'Unità*. Vitorchiano: Monastero di N.S. di S. Giuseppe, 1983.

Sagheddu, Bl. Maria Gabriella. *Cartas desde la Trapa—Beata Ma Gabriella Sagheddu*. Trans. José Antonio Lizondo de Tejada. Burgos, Spain: Editorial Monte Carmelo, 2015.

———. *Lettere dalla Trappa*. Ed. Mariella Carpinello. Milan: Edizioni San Paolo, 2006.

———. *Lettres de la Trappe—Gabriella de l'Unité*. Trans. Claire Boutin. Intro. Mariella Carpinello. Voix Monastique 21. St-Jean-de-Matha: Abbaye Val Notre-Dame Editions, 2010.

Santachiara, Maria Paola. "Madre M. Pia Gullini e Suor Maria Gabriella." *Vita Nostra* 38, no. 2 (2009): 37–52.

———. "Mother Maria Pia Gullini and Sister Maria Gabriella." *Cistercian Studies Quarterly* 47, no. 4 (2012): 407–27.

Schutz, Roger. *The Rule of Taizé*. Taizé: Les Presses de Taizé, 1968.

Simon, Monique. *La vie monastique, lieu oecuménique: Au coeur de l'église-communion*. Paris: Les Éditions du Cerf, 1997.

Sironi, E. M. "Preghiera e conversione all'unità. Il messaggio e la testimonianza di Paul Couturier e Maria Gabriella Sagheddu." *Nicolaus*, Fasc. 1/2, 2000.

Spanu, Dionigi. "La Beata M. Gabriella Sagheddu (1914–1939) nella testimonianza del suo padre spirituale Don Basilio Meloni (1900–1967)." *La palestra del clero* 1, nos. 1–2 (2001): 79–100.

Spreafico, Rosaria. "'Non potrò mai ringraziare abbastanza . . .': La Beata Maria Gabriella Sagheddu: un cammino ecumenico." *L'Osservatore Romano*, 21 April 2002.

Tescari, M. Augusta. "Il carisma di Sr. Maria Gabriella come prassi di vita comunitaria." *Convegno in occasione del 60° anniversario della morte della Beata Maria Gabriella Sagheddu*, Cagliari, Pontifical Theological University of Sardinia, April 23, 1999.

———. "La Beata Maria Gabriella Sagheddu a vent'anni dalla beatificazione." *Vita Nostra* 33, no. 1 (2004).

———. "Madre Pia Gullini, fervente promotrice per l'unità dei cristiani." *L'Osservatore Romano*, 4 July 1999, 5.

———. "Radunare tutti i cristiani nell'unico Regno di Cristo." *L'Osservatore Romano*, 14 January 2000.

———. "Una grande badessa del XX secolo: Madre Pia Gullini." *L'Ulivo, Rivista olivetana di spiritualità e di cultura monastica* 2 (2006): 3–31.

Testore, Celestino. *Suor Maria Gabriella trappista*. Vitorchiano: Monastero di N.S. di S. Giuseppe, 1958.

Unitatis redintegratio: Decree on Ecumenism. www.vatican.va /archive/hist_councils/ii_vatican_council/documents/vat -ii_decree_19641121_unitatis-redintegratio_en.html.

Valtorta, Maria Carla. "Presentation on the Virtues of Sr. Maria Gabriella Sagheddu." Archives of Vitorchiano.

Veilleux, Armand. "Dom Norbert Sauvage: L'art de préparer son successeur." *Collectanea Cisterciensia* 63 (2001): 213–23.

———. "Un grand formateur monastique: Dom Anselme Le Bail." *Collectanea Cisterciensia* 63 (2001): 224–33.

Villain, Maurice. *L'abbé Couturier: Apôtre de l'unité chrétienne*. Paris: Casterman, 1957.

Vogüé, Adalbert de. Preface to *Règles Monastiques au feminin: Dans la tradition de Benoît et Colomban*. Ed. Lazare de Seilhac and M. Bernard Saïd, with M. Madeleine Braquet and Véronique Dupont. Collection Vie Monastique, no. 33. Bégrolles-en-Mauges: Abbaye de Bellefontaine, 1996.

Williamson, Mary Paula. *That All May be One . . . Ut omnes unum sint*. New York: P. J. Kenedy and Sons, 1949.

Zananiri, Gaston. *Dans le mystère de l'Unité: Maria-Gabriella Sagheddu*. 2nd ed. Langres: Dominique Guéniot, 1983.

Contributors

Mariella Carpinello, a scholar of history and monastic spirituality, is the editor of the Italian edition of the *Letters of Blessed Maria Gabriella* and author of the Introduction to this volume. She teaches at the Institute of Theology of Consecrated Life, Pontifical Lateran University-Claretianum. She is on the editorial staff of the reviews *Studia Monastica, L'Ulivo,* and *Nuova Cîteaux*. She has published the following: *Benedetto da Norcia* (Milan: Rusconi, 1991, translated into Spanish as *Libere donne di Dio* (Milan: Mondadori, 1997); translated into French and Portuguese as *Brigida di Svezia* (Casale Monferrato: Edizioni Piemme, 2000); and *Il monachesimo feminile* (Milan: Mondadori, 2002). She has also published extensively in collaboration with other authors. She founded the association *Lettere Dal Monastero* to promote studies on female monasticism, and in 2007 she offered a course on the history of female monasticism at the Pontifical University of Sant'Anselmo in Rome.

David P. Lavich, OCSO, entered the Order of Cistercians of the Strict Observance at Saint Joseph's Abbey in Spencer, Massachusetts, in 1987, after completing twelve years of missionary work in Japan. After solemn profession he was called to serve as chaplain to the Trappistine nuns in Nasu, Japan, to facilitate international meetings of the Order as an interpreter, and to preach retreats in various Asian monasteries. After serving in Rome as a councilor to the abbot general from 2008 until 2017, he has returned as chaplain to the Japanese nuns.

Maria Paola Santachiara, OCSO, entered Abbadia San Giuseppe, Vitorchiano, Viterbo, Italy, on October 7, 1969, and was its prioress from 1978 to 1988 and from 1991 to 2003. She is presently instructor archivist and was Vice Postulatrix of the Cause for the Canonization of Bl. Maria Gabriella until 2013.

Mark A. Scott, OCSO, entered the Order of Cistercians of the Strict Observance at Our Lady of New Clairvaux Abbey, Vina, CA, in 1978. It was there that he composed this article. He was subsequently abbot of Assumption Abbey, Ava, Missouri, and is now abbot of New Melleray Abbey, Peosta, Iowa. Between those two stints in the abbatial service Fr. Mark was for five years editor of *Cistercian Studies Quarterly* and executive editor of Cistercian Publications.

www.ingramcontent.com/pod-product-compliance
Lightning Source LLC
Chambersburg PA
CBHW020108020526
44112CB00033B/1091